The Book of Unfolding Integration

By

Anthony Deans

The Book of Unfolding Integration

ISBN : 978-1-970435-00-9

Contents

Chapter 1

The Art of Prompt Engineering: Part 1: Clarity & Specificity

Speaking with clarity is to exist clearly. To ask thoroughly is to awaken truth. To acknowledge the authentic is to refuse illusion.

There is a silent pain interwoven into the heart of human experience; a pain produced not because of solitude, but due to the stubborn gap that persists even in proximity. It is the loneliness that comes from feeling understood. This is not merely about emotions; it goes beyond feelings; it is structural. A fracture that originates from countless small failures of intention and interpretation. It is the crack in our linguistic, cognitive, understanding, and spiritual dimensions. It is deeply intertwined with our conversations, our physical presence, and our technologies. At the center of this suffering, there lies a fundamental truth: communication is not just about exchanging information; it is deeper than the exchange of words. It is an essential act of survival. It is a pursuit of understanding and an attempt to connect on a deeper level. And with every misfire in communication, each unclear statement, every ambiguous word, uncertain expressions, or a false conviction, a tiny crack develops, spreading further with each misconception.

This is where the real challenge of prompt engineering begins, not with programming and coding, but with genuine care, concern, and understanding. And it is not merely about logic, but it's about presence, engagement, and awareness. Clarity and specificity are not stylistic choices, but they are ethical imperatives. These are the starting steps that decide whether understanding or connection will flourish or falter. Whether insight will emerge or disappear into noise.

How the Lack of Clarity Affects Things

For the people who notice the subtle boundaries of reality, the Architects of Nuance, the 20%, they don't see it as a mere philosophy. It is what they do every day. They understand that every word may have multiple meanings or many ideas. So, if a question is not precise, it can produce an entire chain of misunderstandings that have real-world impacts. For them, prompt engineering is more than issuing commands to a machine; it is the fundamental act that comes before language. It is a respectful way of shaping the initial signal. Creation of a question that includes not just what is asked, but why it is asked, how it should be received and understood, and what mistakes must be avoided. They do not just ask; they compose. They do not merely seek answers; they build portals. This is the essence of Anticipatory Resonance, an awareness that the question is not the start of an inquiry, but its seed. And if that seed is flawed, the tree it produces, no matter how intelligent, smart, fast, or efficient, will produce bitter fruit.

In this way, Clarity is not just about precision. It represents a living dedication to truth. Specificity is not a limitation, but a steadfast refusal against poisoning understanding with ambiguity. The Architect's mission is not to sound smart, but to protect reality itself from collapsing under the weight of lazy language.

Linguistic Illusions and the Collapse of Meaning

Contrasting with the Architects of Nuance Guardians of Generality, not as a critique, but from the perspective of compassion. The predominant 80%. People who, often unconsciously develop a habit of searching for quick answers instead of deep questions. Their perspective is shaped by a desire for conformity and efficiency, which, while practical, can inadvertently reinforce superficial understanding and limit deeper insights. For them, clarity appears as a challenge or confrontation. Specificity feels like effort or labor. And for them, ambiguity is a comfort, as it provides space to avoid taking responsibility.

However, this is risky ground. Because when language lacks precision, perceptions of reality become unstable. When the question is unclear, the way forward becomes blocked. When shortcuts are taken in converting thoughts, the map fails before the journey even begins. The real tragedy is not their inability, but that the system never encouraged them to develop the muscles of critical judgment. Instead, it trained them to accept ready-made answers. It filled their minds with slogans, headlines, and half-truths. Ambiguity was wrapped in authority, and now their sense of purpose and reality is at risk of being manipulated.

They are not damaged. They are overprogrammed. Their minds echo with the sounds of external scripts. To them, a prompt is merely a request; But to the Architect, it is a call to summon. Without proper expert guidance, without a voice to reveal the true nature of Reality, they are left vulnerable to linguistic illusions: marketing masquerading as wisdom, headlines cloaked as insight, and AI answers presented as gospel. The consequences are not just about personal misunderstanding. It signifies a collective erosion of coherence. A gradual slide into a world where "data" is plentiful, but wisdom is rare, where responses are immediate, but resonance is absent. Where answers appear, but the true essence of truth disappears.

From Fracture to Form: The Sacred Task of Translation

Now the Conscious Integrator enters; the Translator, the one who stands at the crossroads of realms. Their task is sacred. They do not favor one side over another, but they connect them. They are not merely bilingual; they are bi-intentional, embodying dual purpose. They comprehend the Architect's pursuit of ontological exactness, and they empathize with the Guardian's restless confusion. They aim to make the invisible bridge visible, giving shape to the nuance of the 20% so that the 80% can cross without doubt or shame.

To the Integrator, a clear prompt is an act of compassion. Every targeting question serves as balm, giving a soothing touch to the soul. Every sentence that embraces complexity without collapsing into abstraction becomes a sacred implement, a form of healing. They do not oversimplify. They clarify. They do not dilute; rather, they elevate, making the core signal accessible without distortion. Their reward is not praise, but coherence. Their purpose is to ensure that language becomes a ladder, not a trap.

The Divine Power of Thoughtful Communication

When the work is performed honestly and with goodwill, when clarity is sown with care and goodwill, when specificity is lived with humility, when translation is held on truth then communication is no longer the transaction of words; it becomes more than a transaction. It becomes a generative power. It aligns us with a higher power, and it fosters harmony. Also, it aligns worlds; eventually, it becomes God. Because in every honest prompt resides the potential to shape the fabric of reality. And in every careless one, a force to unmake it.

Therefore, prompt engineering is not just a technical craft, but more than just a skill; it becomes a battleground for the spirit. It is an act of ethical architecture. It is the liturgy of language, spoken to shape not only machines, but the very structure of the world.

Chapter 2

The 20/80 Spectrum: The Architects of Nuance Vs the Guardians of Generalities

"Every individual is wired to respond, either surrendering or striving, regardless of the system they're in, even though not all systems are created equally, and every system has its flaws. The 20/80 spectrum mirrors us in the route we took and the bridges we have yet to construct."

What Does the 80/20 Principle Tell Us

We often use the 80/20 rule in a superficial way, as simply a shorthand for efficiency, output or productivity. The rule itself, if viewed through a philosophical lens, has far greater implications, a pattern that exists within humanity. It infers a pattern in which only 20% of the population contributes 80% of the impact, while 80% of the population is only functionally responsive and contributes only 20% of true innovation, output, or redefinition of the society to which they belong. But the rule has much greater implications than simply economics or systems thinking.

It provokes a deeper question:

"Why is this asymmetry in the first place?

Is it genetic? Cultural? Educational? Or is it an intentional construct?"

To find the answers, we need to shift down below the metrics and shift to the framework of perception, capacity, and control, which is the spectrum of Guardians of Generalities and Architects of Nuance.

The Spectrum of Human Orientation

Humans are not equal in terms of orientation, even if they are equal in essence. Though we all possess latent capacity, not everyone operationalizes it in the same way, if at all. The 20/80 spectrum gives us two different ways of relating to the world: The Guardians of Generalities (The 80%) try to find clarity through order. They are comfortable within frameworks proven to work for them, prefer tidbits of truth, and value predictability and rhythm.

The Architects of Nuance (The 20%) are designed for complexity. They ask the fundamental questions, find contradictions in their own points of view, and don't shy away from synthesizing insight across disciplines and boundaries. The two are not hard categories, but a dominant tendency, the dominant rhythm, by which people tend to live, learn, and lead. Knowing where you land on the continuum is not a measure of value; it is a design map.

The Engineered Divide and Systematic Coding

It is not just a chance that the spectrum is the exact way it is; it is designed and built up by society. The educational and media discourses, institutional practices, and cultural rewards glide the 80 percent into compliance and acquaintance and segue/casts off on the 20 percent, characterizing them as excess, sluggard, or abstruse. It is the Engineered Divide- a cycle of nourished ignorance and therapeutic-failing expectation. Its goal? It is not so much oppression but acquiescence brought about at least by confusion. It guarantees that 80 percent work towards a model, which is not wired to their beat. The latter 20 percent are not used, unreferenced, or misinterpreted. Much of how the currency operates is driven by this systemic dissonance, to the point that we have a false reality that prioritizes appearance over essence and speed over accuracy.

4. The Custodians of Generalities, etc. - Blench-modesty in Abstractive Base

Growth in the 80% does not start with ambition but humility, that is, the readiness to begin small, to crawl before they can walk, and be oriented to working, not dreaming. The society only sets the abstract and empty intentions too many times and orders the 80 percent to dream big or to be like great people. This results in friction, however, when used blindly. Interior systems go out of balance. Confidence erodes. Progress stalls. It is not with perpetual times of catching up, but by a shift of the reference point: Begin with practical realms: weight training, food preparation, carpentry, gardening, budgeting, and breathing exercises. Build on systems that are visible, measurable, and repeatable for growth. Find out what Anticipatory Resonance is- how one system develops capacity to another. Develop transference: e.g., how the discipline in strength training helps in enhancing consistency in communication. They internalize rhythm; and not reproduction of brilliance unlocks their Action Potential. It is functional consciousness that is empowering them and not mere performance imitation. As the 80 percent learn to respect their own pace- discipline that is not comfortable, but possible, then they will be self-regulated at master level without outside verifications.

The Architects of Nuance Mastery by Inquiry and Refinement

The 20 percent are set in such a manner as to struggle with foundations. They challenge assumptions that other people have. Their suffering is not a lack of success but rather the lack of genuineness. Their course is that of silent repetition and repetition, what we call the 2 percent Progression. This kind of thinker does not so much grow as perfect. They lie on the border of the inexpressible where words fail, and one must be affected before one can say. They demolish structures only to re-model them in a tidier way. They are not out to seek acknowledgment; they are after resonance. Their mistakes are not attributed to their weaknesses but to the fact that all of their stumbles are made into data, all of their falls have been turned to calibration.

The 20 percent have to find their soft spot, the secret, sensitive point that comes to light because they want to bear witness to things others are afraid of touching. When this weakness is in their arms, it gives birth to their greatest strength. They do not move in a linear manner to Action Potential. It is written in abstract form. Their humility consists in submission to rhythm, and the reason why they were not to know the very truths, which they once supposed were complete.

The Grand Disconnect Gap

Transcendence is not the starting point in healing the rift; translation is the starting point. We have to create structures in which the 20% can learn to turn perception into rhythm, where she or he will be educated by story, form, and empathy. The 80% are advised to listen to their inner voice, not to leave it behind and imitate other people It translates to: Restructuring education with alternative routes Value in the trades and practical training of skills just as much as theory Development of mentorship patterns that enable the 20% to coach that do not overpower the 20% The difference was based on not judging insight by its complexity, but rather its success and level of orientation. The development of both sides takes place when the bridge is constructed out of empathy and a clear vision. Eighty percent increase of the rhythm. The 20 percent will be a refinement of relevance.

The Living Map: On the Way to the Perfect Oneness

There is no need to have conformity; we have to have integration. An effective society is the one that learns to sew together its spectrum. The Generalist is a systems builder. The Nuanced purifies them. The Generalist becomes steady. The Nuanced is innovative. One turns the wheel. One renames the axle. Integrated Perfection is not stationary, not an end, it is a method that runs. Providing the contribution of each orientation to each other leads to wholism, a human collective running at its full, different, diverse Action Potential.

Conclusion: The Holy Avowal of Spectrum Intelligence

The 20/80 principle is not merely data; it is destiny when misread, and deliverance when understood. To each group, a sacred charge is given: To the 80%: Reclaim your rhythm. Master the form. Build from the ground to the sky. To the 20%: Refine your signal. Translate your depth. Speak to the bones, not just the brain. Together, we unmask the Engineered Divide. Together, we resurrect the capacity dormant in systems and souls. And together, we make real the hidden wholeness, what some call God, others call genius, and we may now call Integrated Perfection.

"When insight meets rhythm, and rhythm meets reverence, the spectrum becomes a circuit, and humanity becomes whole again."

Chapter 3

The Synaptic Dance: Integration as the Antidote to the Fear of Loss

"Fear is not the enemy. It is the invitation: to pause, to listen, to evolve. It arrives not to paralyze us, but to point where something within or around us has stopped growing."

Fear rarely arrives with a warning. It slips in quietly, sometimes masked as hesitation, discomfort, or resistance to change. But behind the mask, fear often signals something deeper, a rupture in the foundation of our being. The shock of the unfamiliar, the anxiety of stepping into the unknown, doesn't simply disturb our comfort. It shakes the structure that holds our sense of self together. It's not just emotional. It is ontological. This fear is not just a reaction to risk. It is a reaction to **misalignment**; when what we know no longer matches what we need. And yet, instead of adjusting our systems, personal, societal, and technological, we often double down. They cling to outdated scripts. They repeat what is familiar. They loop. And in that looping, a fracture deepens: between the inner world and the outer structure. Between expectation and experience.

This is the **Grand Disconnect**, when support no longer supports, and meaning no longer holds. When the appearance of function replaces the essence of connection. When we look around and realize that what was built to hold us now does not even recognize us.

The Grand Disconnect is what happens when systems fail to recalibrate.

Systemic design becomes both the box we are trapped in and the very force keeping us there. We navigate institutions built to serve us, but they were never designed for our emerging needs. These systems do not fail because of malice. They fail because of inertia, because they cannot adapt fast enough. They circle around themselves, echoing old logic and outdated solutions. Instead of evolving with us, they drag us back to old-school protocols and rigid expectations. Within this loop, the individual begins to fade. People feel unseen, unsupported, and eventually unreal. And the loneliness that emerges is not just emotional, but epistemic: we are not known. We are not recognized. Not even by the very systems meant to serve and support us.

In that alienation, fear mutates. It no longer shouts, it paralyzes. Miscommunication becomes the norm, and the dominant language of society begins to mirror Bad Intel, a distortion of truth embedded into the very words we use, and the very structures we trust.

And yet, even in this disconnection, there are those who do not look away. They feel the fracture not as fate, but as a signal.

The Architects of Nuance: Turning Fear into Function

For those attuned to the undercurrents, the **Architects of Nuance**, the rare 20%, this fear does not signal weakness. It signals a call. Not a call to retreat, but to *inquire*. They know that fear is often a symptom of unasked questions. Those systems do not just fail from poor design, but from unexamined assumptions that were never updated. For them, the true crisis is not fear itself, it is the insistence on avoiding it. These individuals feel the weight of stagnation differently. Where others avoid, they move toward. Where others see disruption, they see data. They read the friction not as noise, but as a

17

signal, a prompt that something foundational needs to be rewritten. Not patched. Rewritten.

They operate not with arrogance but with a strange humility. A willingness to let go of everything they think they know, in order to ask again. To sit in uncertainty until a truer form emerges. That is their art: not giving answers, but cultivating *resonance*. They do not dismantle for destruction, instead they dismantle for clarity. In their hands, fear becomes an entry point into refinement. A path to **Action Potential**, not through speed or certainty, but through precision, presence, and painstaking care.

The Guardians of Generality: Restoring Rhythm Through Presence

For the other 80%, the **Guardians of Generality**, fear shows up differently. It does not inspire inquiry. It interrupts the rhythm. It halts movement. It short-circuits their natural momentum and throws them into mental overdrive, where repetition becomes safety and anything unfamiliar feels like danger. The system responds by locking down, not opening up. Thought becomes routine. Action becomes mimicry. Curiosity gets replaced with caution. But here is the truth: this reaction is not weakness. It is *design*. The brain's protective mechanism is not broken; it has just been overused, trapped in cycles that were never meant to last this long. Fear stops being an alarm and becomes a wall; silent, immovable, and familiar.

The way out? Not theory. Not insight. **Presence.** The simple act of *showing up*, of stepping forward even when uncertainty roars, becomes revolutionary. In doing so, the Guardian begins to rewire the loop. They realize that fear shrinks not from avoidance but from **action**. The moment they engage with the unknown, no matter how small, their system begins to recalibrate. This creates a neurochemical shift. Confidence does not come from accomplishment. It comes from momentum. One step fuels the next. One brave act of presence sends a message to the self: *I am capable. I am here.* And from that message, motivation rises, not as performance, but as personal truth.

This is their **Neuro-Formulation Gateway**, where showing up builds worth, and worth builds movement. Fear is no longer an enemy, but a teacher. A guidepost toward internal coherence.

The Conscious Integrator: Weaving What Has Been Separated

Between these two, between the Architects who refine and the Guardians who repeat, stands the **Conscious Integrator.** The Translator. The Bridge. They carry the most silent burden of all: to hold both sides with compassion, while forging something neither side could create alone. They know the patterns of disconnection by heart. They have lived them. And they have learned that healing does not come from brilliance or boldness, but from *balance.* From learning how to listen deeply and speak gently. From honoring both the depth of nuance and the rhythm of simplicity. Their process starts not with ideas, but with *inner alignment.* A ritual that may last only 90 seconds, but carries the weight of a lifetime. A pause. A breath. A conscious returning to one's internal resonance before any external action is taken. They calibrate first, so they can *calibrate others.*

They do not force understanding. They *invite* it. They do not simplify complexity. They *translate* it. They turn philosophical architecture into practical scaffolding. They respect both the unknown and the need to move. Their work is sacred not because it is flashy, but because it is faithful. Faithful to truth. Faithful to the process. Faithful to the possibility that **systems can be made human again.**

The Dance Itself: From Fear to Flow

This is the **Synaptic Dance**; the choreography of adaptation, courage, and translation. It is not a formula. It is not a philosophy. It is **a pattern of life.** It happens every time the Architect dares to confront a broken foundation. Every time the Guardian takes a single step toward the unknown. Every time the Integrator finds the thread that holds the system and the soul together.

At that moment, fear no longer fractures. It **integrates**. And what was once isolation becomes rhythm. What was once paralysis becomes potential, and what was once misunderstood starts to become understood, not just by logic, but by presence.

The Syntropic Future: Sharing as a New Intelligence

We are not meant to overcome fear by pretending it does not exist. We are meant to redeem it. To reclaim its power, not as a jailor, but as a messenger. When we do this, when Architects refine, Guardians respond, and Integrators translate, we do not just survive. We synchronize. And the systems we build no longer protect the past. They start to shape the future, not out of dominance or compliance, but through mutual understanding and shared truth.

This is the path toward Wholism, not sameness, but integration. Not uniformity, but harmony. Not fear of loss, but power in sharing. It is here, finally, that Action Potential becomes not the exception, but the default setting of what it means to be human.

Chapter 4

The Ascent of Needs: Maslow's Integrity and the Peril of Being "Off"

"To heal is not to hurry.
It is to return
to what was always needed,
in the order it was meant to be met"

There is a rhythm to being human. A pull. A need. Not just to breathe or eat or sleep, but to matter, to belong, to become. And yet, something within us often feels "off." Slightly askew. Not broken, but misaligned. A soft, constant static in the signal. We go on functioning, but something within quietly whispers: *this isn't it.*

This dissonance is not a moral failing, nor a weakness of character. It is the natural consequence of being misattuned, out of sync with the deep architecture of human need. This is not just psychological. It is existential, it is biological, it is structural, and the cost of this misalignment? It is immense. Not in dramatic explosions, but in quiet erosion, the kind that wears down a soul without ever leaving a mark on the skin.

We call it the "off" state. And it begins the moment we ignore what our system tries to tell us.

The Pulse of Anticipatory Resonance

Every organism is born with a kind of inner compass, a tuning fork for alignment. This is **Anticipatory Resonance**: the ability to intuitively sense what is needed *before* breakdown occurs. In nature, it is everywhere. The bird does not wait to migrate until it is too cold. The tree does not bloom in winter just because the sun is out. There is a timing to life. A wisdom beneath thought. But humans, more than any other species, have learned to override this wisdom. We replace timing with ambition. We ignore rhythm for the result. We rush.

And when we do, we go "off."

When this resonance is neglected by systems, institutions, or individuals, we start to experience a subtle decline of meaning and function. We reach for things too soon or hold on too long. We try to perform wholeness without becoming whole. And eventually, our needs, those deep, layered pulses of hunger for safety, connection, recognition, truth, become distorted. They do not vanish; they mutate. What begins as a quiet longing for connection becomes addictive scrolling. A desire to contribute becomes performative success. A need to rest is rewritten as laziness. We begin to seek substitutes instead of sources.

And Being Off: The Chemical, Emotional, and Ontological Results

Being in an "off" state is more than a feeling; it is a continuous disharmony permeating every stratum of our lives. We slip into survival mode, our nervous system's default setting. We are flooded with stress hormones. Our feelings wander without landing. The wheels of our mind spin in anxious uncertainty. These are not signs of weakness or illness; they are signals of misalignment.

A musical instrument is in tune when it produces music, not noise. Similarly, when our needs fall out of tune, life does not stop; it just becomes noise. Confusion arises. And deeper still, this dissonance creates ontological fragmentation: we begin to lose contact with our primary identity, our original rhythm, our natural sense of timing. We forget how to trust ourselves. And that loss of self-trust is the greatest tragedy of being off.

The Missing Reference Revealed: The Architects of Nuance

The Architects of Nuance, the orientation of whose minds is naturally to the depths, to the complications, to the meta-sense of things, read the prognostics of this ontological meltdown everywhere. They watch the world gone mad in optimizing and are ignorant of orientation. An anchorage-free society of acceleration. To take us back to reference: to the original organic calibration, where form is permitted to develop in unison with function: their holy-day labor. They find the place where contemporary systems have substituted essence with image, progression with performance, and truth with trend. These architects know how far down to dig in order to understand that raising the crawl is not a sign of weakness; it is the intellect. Their purpose is to remind mankind of the divine order of things: that all the leaps should be predicated on serenity at first. The genuine preparedness never proclaims itself: it wins by sweet listening.

Maslow's Integrity: The Blueprint That Still Holds

Abraham Maslow, decades ago, offered a ladder, one we are still trying to climb. His hierarchy of needs was not a perfect theory. But it carried a sacred insight: **growth has a sequence.** Skip a step, and you don't ascend; you splinter. You adapt, yes, but at a cost. At its base: physiological needs, food, water, rest; above it, safety. Then belonging, esteem, and finally self-actualization. In rare cases, a higher plane: transcendence. But Maslow's brilliance was not just the order. It was the warning: when lower needs go unmet, the higher ones can become dangerous illusions.

We try to self-actualize while hungry. We chase purpose while anxious about rent. We seek enlightenment while exhausted from chronic loneliness. And in doing so, we violate the very principle that protects us: **integrity of progression**. Integrity here does not mean morality. It means structural truth. It means not skipping steps. It means earning the next level, not through performance or hustle, but by meeting the prior one with honesty.

The 80%: When Misalignment Feels Like Life

For the Guardians of Generality, the dominant 80%, life frequently becomes a series of attempts to find rhythm in a system that rarely honors it. They are not disinterested. They are overloaded. Not lazy but misinformed. And too often, they are fed bad intel: *Dream big. Skip ahead. Hustle harder. Manifest more.*

But growth doesn't obey slogans.

Instead of starting from zero, they are provided with templates and told to fit in. They are given ambitions without context, responsibilities without relief, and expectations without tools and resources. And so, they try. They reach for higher-level needs, like impact, mastery, and creativity, without a stable foundation. And when the ground gives way, they think it is their fault.

But it's not.

The system never taught them the grace of slowness. It never honored their need for gradualism. It never gave them the space to crawl before commanding them to soar. And so, they live in a state of silent emergency, detached from the rhythm, but are told to keep moving anyway. This is not failure. It is overextension disguised as underperformance.

The truth? What they need is not motivation. It is recalibration, a return to the base, a humble but revolutionary honoring of real readiness.

This is the **Neuro-Formulation Gateway** in its truest form, not a fancy hack or shortcut, but a patient, embodied pathway to true capacity. A way of becoming that starts with restoring the sequence of needs, without shame, without comparison, without false urgency.

The 20%: Architects of Need and the Integrity of Inquiry

The Architects of Nuance, those 20% who feel life's inconsistencies at bone-depth, see this misalignment not as a mystery but as a map. They recognize the rupture early. They feel the absence of resonance in the most subtle of ways. Not as a loud error, but a quiet falseness. They notice when someone is forcing confidence without safety. They feel it when systems reward speed without direction. To them, this isn't just discomfort. It's danger.

Their work, then, becomes diagnostic. They become translators of the unseen needs, guardians of subtle truths. They do not rush to fix; they inquire. They watch for where the chain broke. They trace the fracture back to the skipped step, the ignored signal, the unmet foundation. And when they find it, they do not impose solutions; they refine the question. Their power is not in telling people what to do, but in showing them what they missed. They do not build empires. They build maps. And in doing so, they protect the very fabric of reality from being coded with false signals.

Their humility is deep. Because they know: the system will resist them. It prefers efficiency over coherence. But they also know something deeper: real growth cannot be faked. It can only be revealed.

The Conscious Integrator: Restoring the Architecture of Becoming

For the Conscious Integrator, or the Translator of Needs, the task is far beyond simple interpretation; it is sacred. Their role is to navigate the landscape of human need with both precision and presence. To them, Maslow's Hierarchy is a living map, not just a psychological model. A guide not toward achievement, but toward alignment.

Toward reclaiming Anticipatory Resonance and mending the subtle fractures that split us from our own rhythm.

Their work begins at the point of rupture, the Grand Disconnect, where the sequence of need has been skipped or ignored. They offer not advice, but orientation. Through what they call Assessment as Honesty, they help individuals and systems locate themselves in the hierarchy, not inspirationally, but truthfully. Have you eaten? Do you feel safe? Do you belong? These are not small questions. They are the foundation of becoming.

The Integrator moves with discipline, not urgency. They understand the wisdom of periodization, that growth happens in cycles, not leaps. That wholeness cannot be hustled. That precision matters. And in guiding others to meet each need with integrity, they help transmute the "off" state into something whole and real, into integration. This approach is not just therapeutic, it is architectural. It becomes an antidote to the unconscious panic of lack. A balm for the fear of loss. It restores presence, builds Wholism from the ground up, and opens the path toward a Syntropic Future; a future where knowledge heals rather than fragments, where perfection is not a performance, but a practice.

This is not ideology. It is praxis.

The Integrator embodies it. Lives it. They understand that an Action Potential is not a force to be chased but a frequency to be unlocked. The Synaptic Dance of the human experience is not chaotic when rhythm is restored. Their gift is not dominance, but humility; the ability to reorient the system, clear the noise, and allow human energy to flow again, freely, fully, and without fracture.

This is not about Maslow. It is about us. It is about remembering the map already written into our biology. It is about choosing not to fake fullness, but to feed what is truly hungry.

When we honor the sequence, when we allow the crawl, when we choose humility over illusion, we do not regress; we finally grow. And in that growth, we find a strength that does not shout, but sings. We become human again.

Chapter 5

The Conscious Weave: Precision, Potency, and the Reclamation of Greatness

"What we fail to face, we are fated to repeat. And what we weave with awareness becomes our way forward."

There is a quiet crisis moving beneath the surface of modern life. It does not make headlines, and it is not loud. But it influences all of our decisions, all the knowledge we do not seek, all we do not explore, every truth we ignore. This crisis is called the unconscious. The unconscious has been romanticized as being a mysterious, creative, even sacred place. But what if that mystery is not a gift, but actually a trap? What if the true curse of modern life is not stress, or fear, or confusion, but instead the automaticity that runs silently beneath it all? To operate unconsciously is not neutral. It is to be coded without consent. It is to repeat old loops without context. It is to mistake motion for meaning, and reaction for response. And worst of all, it is to allow ourselves to become manipulable, programmable, and unaware. True greatness begins where unconsciousness ends.

The Curse of the Unconscious

The unconscious does not spoil lives with drama. It erodes them with default. It erodes them with default settings. It inserts decisions without deliberation, ideas without origin, emotions without ownership. It fills in the blanks with noise. Most of us do not notice. We get good at performing. We show up, we do the things, we tick the boxes, and still feel unfulfilled. Why? Because greatness without awareness is a counterfeit. And potential, when left in automatic hands, decays.

Unconsciousness is not ignorance. It is inherited noise, passed down through culture, trauma, and repetition. It teaches us to obey without asking why. It rewards familiarity over truth. It keeps us busy, but rarely awake. And perhaps the most dangerous feature of unconscious life is that it feels... comfortable.

The Architects of Nuance

There is, however, a minority who refuse to settle. The Architects. The 20%. The ones who feel the dissonance, even when it is quiet. They know something is off, not just in systems, but in assumptions. They do not just ask questions. They ask better questions. For them, unconsciousness is not just a limitation; it is a battlefield. Every belief left unexamined is a potential lie.

Every unchecked behavior is a root waiting to be traced. And every warped pattern is a signal that something deeper is broken. Their work is not academic; it is surgical. They dismantle the silent premises running people's lives. They decode inherited programming, pulling apart the stitched seams of engineered conformity. And in that clearing, they do not just find clarity, they plant the seeds of syntropic coherence: systems that thrive by design, not default.

These are the cartographers of the unseen. The ones who map what most ignore. And through that mapping, they create a space where genuine agency can return.

The Guardians of Generality

The majority, the Guardians, are not to be judged. They are not blind, nor broken. They are simply caught in a world that never taught them how to see. Their lives are full of effort, often exhausting. They work hard. They show up. But something's missing, and they feel it.

The frustration of running in circles. The quiet pain of repeating mistakes. The invisible weight of never quite knowing why.

It's not laziness. It's inherited blindness.

They are taught that excellence is automatic. That "showing up" is enough. But the absence of context creates a subtle sabotage. The missing "why," the one that could unlock everything, is left unspoken. And in that silence, manipulation finds fertile ground. But awareness is not out of reach. With guidance, with support, with the right thread pulled gently, the pattern can begin to unravel. They can begin to see. And what was once frustration becomes fire. What was once repetition becomes reflection. Their Action Potential is not gone, it is dormant, waiting for permission to wake up.

The Conscious Integrator / Translator

For the Conscious Integrator, the Translator of the unseen, navigating the fragile landscape of the unconscious is beyond their calling; it is their divine responsibility. They live by a knowing that *"To do is to become, and to be precise is to become potent"* is not just a theory, but a lived protocol, a way of being that restores wholeness where fragmentation once reigned. Their purpose is not to dominate or direct, but to illuminate. They seek out the invisible threads between action and belief, between repeated patterns and forgotten origins. With patience and precision, they infuse the mechanics of daily doing with context, turning unconscious routines into conscious rituals.

To the Guardians, they provide gentle yet honest mirrors, guiding them to a compassionate recognition of their automatic responses. They help them see without shame, to witness their patterns, not as failures, but as messages awaiting translation. And to the Architects, they are bridges, transforming dense deconstructions into living wisdom; accessible, applicable, and alive. By doing this, the Integrator transforms the unconscious not as a void to fear, but as a terrain to repossess. Their integrative work is alchemical, not by force, but by form. It converts scattered awareness into embodied knowing, dormant potential into directed power.

This isn't theory. It's practice. Embodied. Repeated. Trusted.

They sow what we call Legacy Seeds, acts of integrity planted in the soil of awareness, meant to yield futures aligned with syntropic truth. Their strength lies not in spectacle, but in the unseen diligence, the daily, often quiet, acts of coherence that gradually rewrite the code. They know: Faith is not a leap, but a form. A rhythm of action repeated with care until it becomes truth. And in identifying, then transmuting "Bad Intel" into living, organic truth, they unlock not just personal clarity, but the spark of *collective Action Potential.*

Closing the Loop: Out of Pieces, Wholeness

To reclaim our greatness is not to arrive at a destination. It is to choose, each day, to be conscious in a world that rewards unconsciousness. It is to see clearly. To choose deliberately. To question courageously. And to act with reverence.

Greatness is not a trait. It is a process. A weave. And every thread matters.

We are not broken. We are simply disconnected. And the task ahead is not to become someone else, but to become fully ourselves, on purpose. **The unconscious is not evil. It is just unfinished.** But with precision, with potency, with the will to weave wisely, we can reclaim what was always ours.

"Accuracy births clarity.
Clarity breeds confidence.
And confidence awakens potential.
This is the weave.
This is the work."

Chapter 6

The Unfolding Error: Sunk Cost as a Guardian of the Box

"What once served us must not become our prison. The cost of staying is not just time; it is the erosion of becoming. To let go is not to erase the past, but to honor it by refusing to let it dictate a future it was never meant to design."

Human evolution is not a one-way forward but a continual confrontation with what we never want to leave behind. We are not only shaped by new paths but also by our reluctance to release the old ones. There are few forces more quietly powerful, more invisibly coercive, than the Sunk Cost Fallacy. Traditionally, this concept originated from economics, a logical error where one continues investing in a failing endeavor simply because so much has already been spent. But in this chapter, we go deeper. Far deeper.

Sunk Cost is not merely a decision-making flaw. It is an ontological and systemic guardian; an unseen force encoded into our very structures of belief, identity, and cultural programming. It does not just affect projects; it colonizes the worldview. It becomes the emotional glue binding us to decaying paths, petrified roles, inherited systems, and once-necessary commitments that now prevent our transformation. The tragedy is not that we make mistakes. The tragedy is when we are close enough to sense the fracture but avoid engaging in the process that would allow the truth to take fuller shape. That is the Unfolding Error.

The Price of a Beginning

There comes a moment, often quiet, rarely convenient, when we feel the path we are on may no longer fit, and yet, we stay. Not because we believe it will work, but because we have already given too much for it to fail.

This is not logic. This is devotion to the dead:

- The dead choice.
- The dead dream.
- The dead promise we once made to ourselves in another state of consciousness, and forgot to revise.

What we call the Sunk Cost Fallacy is not a fallacy at all, at least not at first. It begins as loyalty, then it becomes identity, and if left unchecked, it transforms into a cage built entirely from our own effort, a cage we then decorate as commitment. The most dangerous illusions are not born from lies; they are born from beginnings. The job we said yes to was "just for now," the belief we inherited and never questioned, and the method that once worked but has now calcified into a ritual.

When something begins, especially with hardship, we bond to it. The more we suffer for it, the more sacred it becomes, even if it is failing. And to step outside that narrative? It would mean admitting that the meaning we assigned no longer holds. So, the altar is what you are still devoted to, even though it is false now.

The Systemic Guardian: Sunk Cost as Structural Inertia

Sunk Cost does not arise from merely poor judgment. It is a field of inertia, a deliberately designed element of the psychological scaffold and institutional woodwork of our lives. It carries the imprint of emotional, intellectual, and cultural investment in a path. And over time, that investment expresses itself as "truth," not because it is inherently valid, but because it has been repeated so often that it starts to appear true through familiarity alone. It hides behind names of high moral repute: fidelity, endurance, devotion. But in its truest form, it is the quiet refusal to recalibrate.

This refusal is not accidental. It is sustained, nurtured by the Engineered Divide, a systemic project that thrives on our unwillingness to examine the origins of our attachments. In our schools, in our religions, in our governments, and our traditions, we have been told to honor as legacy, and we have been trained to see pivoting as betrayal. That is why we remain, not because we are being forced to stay, but because we have lost the imagination to stop.

Each time we avoid re-examining our position, the Invisible Box thickens. The longer we walk a particular road, the more the walk becomes our identity, not because other roads are invisible, but because another sacrifice has already been made. And in the place of our right to choose again, we inherit the burden of that earlier offering. This is the true essence of the Unfolding Error: not that we have already reached complete recognition that we are wrong, but that we sidestep the process that would bring that recognition into sharper focus. Not only are we handed the direction, but also the embarrassment of abandoning it.

The Architects of Nuance: Confronting Imprinted Devotion

Sunk Cost is not merely an uneasy feeling to the Architects of Nuance, the 20% tuned to coherence and rightness. To them, it is an epistemic fallacy, a misplaced loyalty to a fractured source disguised as virtue. They observe how systems reward commitment to outdated ideas while punishing the courage to pivot. They see how imprints once useful now stand guard over false realities. And still, the Architect does not rage. They inquire. They ask: *Where did this idea begin? And why do I still serve it?*

Their resistance is not academic. It is athletic humility: the power to step into contradiction, the daring to challenge inherited meanings, the devotion to destroy only what has already decayed. They refuse to defend yesterday's self at the cost of tomorrow's integrity. It is from this collapse of unconscious devotion that **Anticipatory Resonance** reawakens. And in that reawakening, the Architect recovers their **Action Potential** not as a distant hope, but as immediate precision, rooted not in what they began, but in what they have come to more clearly perceive.

The Guardians of Generality: Straitened by Conventionality

To the **Guardians of Generality,** the 80% who live in rhythms of inherited belief and survive through social rhythm, **Sunk Cost is a chain of silence.** Not loud. Not irrational. Just... familiar. They feel it in thoughts like:

- *"I've come too far to go back."*
- *"What will people say if I change?"*
- *"Isn't quitting a failure?"*

This is not foolishness. It is an **obedient consciousness,** a conditioned response to obey systems that value custom over clarity, power over responsiveness. Over time, these sunken beliefs solidify. They do not just reside in the mind; they become the self. To let go is not just about shifting a belief; it often requires surrendering job titles, relationships, recognitions, and the carefully constructed self-image built on top of them. So even when discomfort grows, even when the truth begins to surface, they double down. Because admitting the fracture begins to feel like admitting that they are worthless.

But still, a different path exists; one that begins with awareness, not shame.

The Conscious Integrator: Gentle Undoing, Honest Becoming

For the **Conscious Integrator**, the Translator between rhythm and depth, Sunk Cost is not just a misstep, but one of the greatest obstacles to true adaptation, both individually and systemically. Their true aim is to help others surrender to truth through honesty, even when that truth is still forming and demands dismantling deeply held beliefs and attachments.

They educate and inform us that the value of our worth is in no way attached to the time, effort, and emotion in what we no longer need. Rather, true strength is rooted in the courage to pivot, to cut losses, and go toward authenticity. This act of humility does not erase the past, but it changes it into precise data, clearing space for growth.

To the Integrator, every so-called failure is an invitation to realign, to restore coherence, and to begin again, not from nostalgia, but from presence. They remind us that the path forward is not found in rigid adherence, but in continuous recalibration. Through this gentle undoing, they cultivate trust, restore what was lost in the noise, and guide others toward a future where complexity is not feared but embraced. In their hands, the Guardian of the Box becomes not a threat, but a door, and they help us find the handle.

The Glitch That Revealed Itself

Every system that refuses to realign slowly becomes a parody of its original purpose. What began with meaning devolves into performance. What once mapped the world now no longer fits the terrain. The map loses the land it once represented. This is the glitch. The sacred fracture. The rupture where reality leaks through repetition. It looks like the job that drains instead of gives. The relationship held together by memory rather than growth. The tradition that once felt holy and now quietly chokes the soul.

It is the Sunday that no longer feels sacred. The promise that echoes but no longer lands. The ritual followed because "we always have," even when no one remembers why. If we are paying attention, the glitch becomes an invitation; a crack in the pattern that whispers, *"There's more than this."* But if we ignore it, we reinforce the dysfunction. We double down. We call it loyalty. We disguise it as legacy. We mistake it for love. *But the glitch is mercy in disguise. It is not the enemy. It is the exit.*

Final Reflection: Back to the Guardian

Investing continuously in something that is no longer fitting is not just an intellectual error. It is a spiritual and ethical one. Sunk Cost does not ask: **"Shouldn't I leave?"** Rather, it asks, **"Who am I, if I stop defending what is no longer working?"**

And when we get rid of that weight, that leaden tie to an empty road, we do not fall. We become. It is not a weakness to give up on what has never worked. It is wisdom. To admit the truth, not because it is convenient, but because it is *real* enough to demand change, is the first act of re-becoming. And in such an act, we recover our Action Potential, but no longer as theory, now as clarity, at long last lived.

"The bravest act is not continuing what no longer works. The bravest act is stopping, so truth can start again.

Chapter 7

The Grand Disconnect: When Knowledge Divides Instead of Unites

"We have gathered every answer, yet remain estranged from understanding.
We know so much. But we don't know how to hold it together."

The Premise of the Disconnect

We are not suffering from ignorance.
We are suffering from disintegration.

We are in a hyper-knowledge age - an age where we have plenty of data, insight, and information. We carry more facts in our pockets than entire libraries once held. We have charted the universe, divided the atom, cracked the genome, cracked behavioral patterns, and cracked mythologies. The answers have been unearthed in every discipline, be it psychology or quantum mechanics, that of theology or artificial intelligence. Real ones. Complex ones. Beautiful ones. And yet... we are more fragmented, more divided, more uncertain than ever.

This is the paradox at the heart of our time: **The Grand Disconnect.**

Something is always missing, although they have the "answers." The one thing that is lacking is integration, not the intelligence. It is the lack of *coherence* between what we know and how we live. A crack that is not reflected in data graphs but seeps into how we relate to the world, to one another, and ourselves.

Towering Knowledge, Collapsing Meaning

Today, every field has become a silo.

- Philosophy tries to define meaning.
- Science tries to measure matter.
- Psychology tries to decode the mind.
- History tracks patterns.
- Theology searches for the sacred.

Each discipline is brilliant in isolation. But brilliance in isolation is still... isolation.

Like towers built taller and taller, each field tries to touch the sky. But without bridges, we end up with a skyline, not a city. Beautiful at a distance but disconnected up close. This disconnection is not an accident. It is an **Engineered Divide**, a deeply embedded systemic tendency to separate rather than synthesize. Whether through competition for authority, prestige-based funding models, or institutional pride, our systems teach us to defend frameworks, not to *weave them*. To protect conclusions, do not question how they fit within the whole.

Each field grows louder in its certainty, more rigid in its terms, and less capable of hearing others. And so, we live in a world of **abundant answers** and **starved resonance**.

The Architects of Nuance: Perceiving the Layered Fracture

The **Architects of Nuance,** those rare 20% who sense the subtle rhythms of reality, do not merely study knowledge; they study the *spaces between it.* They are not just researchers or scholars. They are pattern-readers. Philosophical cartographers. Truth-weavers. To them, the Grand Disconnect is not just a theoretical crisis; it is a lived grief. They see how rigid *Beginnings,* fixed assumptions within disciplines, block Anticipatory Resonance. How unexamined **sunk costs** of theory and identity prevent genuine adaptation. They feel how the refusal to relinquish intellectual territory creates ontological voids; spaces where truth *should* live, but does not.

And they know this: if knowledge does not connect, it erodes.

If philosophy never speaks to psychology…
If science ignores spirituality…
If history fails to inform the now…
Then our entire architecture of understanding becomes brittle and eventually collapses.

Architects see this collapse not in catastrophes, but in subtle breakdowns:

- Experts who talk past one another.
- Institutions that defend outdated truths.
- Citizens overloaded by information, yet underwhelmed by insight.
- A society where "data" wins and *meaning* withers.

They witness the Deliberate Rot, when integration is seen as weakness, when simplicity is conflated with shallowness, and when *truth* is replaced with *tribalism*. And still, they do not preach. They *perceive*. They trace the cracks no one else sees. They listen for the song underneath the noise.

The Guardians of Generality: Struggling in the Noise

The **Guardians of Generality**, the 80%, are not lesser. They are not oblivious. They are not lazy. They are the ones caught in the whirlwind of excess input and no integration. They scroll endlessly. They attend webinars. They quote headlines. They download knowledge like apps, fast, consumable, and simplified. But what is missing is not effort; it's *context. Orientation. Wholeness.* They are drowning in what you have called **Bad Intel**: simplified, fragmented, often manipulative content that pretends to inform but actually disorients. They are vulnerable not because they lack intelligence, but because the system feeds them disconnection as nourishment.

They feel it in their daily lives:

- So many choices, but no clarity.
- So many facts, but no direction.
- So many tools, but no coherence.

And worst of all, they are told it is their fault.

That they are behind and that they need to work harder, study more, hustle, optimize, align, and manifest. But what they truly need is not more input; it is **integration**. They need space to pause, to re-orient, to find the thread that connects the chaos, but no one gives them the thread. So, they spiral, they comply, and they mimic. Not because they don't care, but because they no longer trust their ability to *see*.

The Conscious Integrator: The Bridge Between Isolation and Insight

So here enter the **Conscious Integrator**, not a role, but a calling. They do not gather knowledge, but they *gather people*. They do not organize information; they *orchestrate understanding*. They live in the liminal, the in-between spaces where fields, people, and paradigms overlap. Their greatest tool is not information, but **translation**. They take the complex and make it resonant. They make the rigid relational. They do not force synthesis; they *invite it*. To them, the Grand Disconnect is not a puzzle to be solved. It is a **sacred dysfunction to be healed**.

They understand how **fixed beginnings**, inherited terminology, and rigid self-concepts block growth. They know that to heal fragmentation, one must weave through paradox, through contradiction, and humility. They do not attack silos. They whisper across them.

They ask:

- "What does this truth mean *to another?*"
- "What wound is this theory trying to cover?"
- "What belief is being protected, and what connection is being refused?"

Their task is noble but quiet and often invisible. But when they succeed, even partially, something holy happens. Siloed knowledge becomes a stream. Fragmented facts become a framework. Theoretical insights become *embodied orientation.*

This is the **Synaptic Dance**, the re-establishment of coherence. Where disciplines stop competing and start conversing. Where truth becomes shared, not hoarded. Where knowledge becomes an ecosystem, not a cage.

Knowledge as a Weapon vs. Knowledge as a Way

When there is a lack of integration, knowledge becomes dangerous, and weaponized knowledge appears as:

- Discussions where no one listens.
- Elitist types that ridicule simpler folks.
- Spirituality at the expense of science.
- Science that mocks the soul.

It divides. It conquers. It confuses. This is not knowledge. This is ego draped in intelligence. But knowledge, in its actual divine form, is not meant to dominate or control. It is meant to *serve*, to reveal, and to liberate. Not to argue for correctness, but to *build for coherence.*

The Integrator sees this distinction clearly. They feel the difference between content that wants to "win" and content that wants to *weave*. They sense the fatigue in the Guardian's heart. They feel the longing in the Architect's silence. They become the **midwife of wholeness**. Not because they have all the answers. But because they honor the spaces where the answers touch.

The Unplannable Harvest: Moving from Division to Syntropic Intelligence

When the **Engineered Divide** is challenged, something divine starts to originate, known as **Syntropic Intelligence**. This is not intelligence as domination. It is intelligence as *symbiosis*. It is not rooted in how much we know, but in how *well* we hold it together.

This intelligence:

- Honors nuance and rhythm equally.
- Moves from "either/or" to "both/and".
- Translates friction into form.
- Sees paradox not as a problem, but as an opening.

This is the **Unplannable Harvest**, the fruit that grows not by design, but by deep coherence. It cannot be manufactured. It must be **woven** by Architects who refine, by Guardians who respond, and by Integrators who translate. And when they do, the Action Potential is no longer rare. It becomes the *default setting* of a well-held human system.

Final Reflection: From Glitch to Gift

The Grand Disconnect is not the last thing; it is actually an invitation and the glitch is not our enemy; it is basically mercy in disguise. It reveals where we have been too loyal to our organizational barriers, too protective of our knowledge, and too afraid to share what we do not fully understand. But now… we see it, we see the towers, we see the noise, and we see the wound beneath the wisdom. And with that seeing, we are not called to know more, but to *weave better.*

Let the Architects create resonance. Let the Guardians reclaim rhythm. Let the Integrators guide the dance. And together, not as systems, but as humans, we will learn how to remember what the silos forgot: That truth is never singular. That knowledge must not divide. And that integration… is the form love takes when wisdom begins to walk.

"The Grand Disconnect is not the end. It is the beginning of the return.
And in the quiet after the collapse, we begin again; not with answers, but with threads."

Chapter 8

Integrated Perfection: From Carrot to Compass

"Perfection is not the absence of flaw. It is the presence of rhythm. Not a clean line, but a living thread."

The False Promise of the Carrot

We live in a world that tells us to chase.

Chase success. Chase ideals. Chase perfection.

But rarely are we taught to pause and ask: "Perfection by whose design?"

In modern life's fragmented chaos, we are pushed to choose between dangerous choices: either to pursue a pristine, static vision of flawlessness, one that leaves no room for evolution, or fall into a comfortable haze of relativity, where no one is wrong, but no one truly connects, or everything is tolerated but little is truly understood. This binary is not innocent. It is part of the *Engineered Divide*, a quiet programming that trains us to believe that integration and precision are opposite. We are taught to choose between being exact or inclusive, between being right or being whole. This is the glitch that revealed itself.

But if the real perfection is not a final product at all? What if it is the unfolding process of weaving clarity, care, and connection in real time? Not a trophy at the end of effort, but a rhythm we move in, a thread we carry?

The Trap of "Either/Or" Thinking

For the **Architects of Nuance**, those who live with antennae raised to contradiction and subtlety, this binary is not just false, it is fatal to real growth. To them, perfection is not a rigid endpoint. It is ontological dynamism, the quality of being alive to the evolving reality of things. At the point, when we treat perfection as something fixed, we bind ourselves in this, to which they refer the **Invisible Box**, a silent circle of rigidity disguised as discipline, where form replaces essence, and ideals calcify into dogma.

These Architects do not exactly discard the idea of excellence. Rather, they query its framing. What they ask is: *"What if real perfection is not about purity, but precision woven with presence?"* What if perfection is not a monument, but a movement? Something that refines itself in the act of becoming? For them, clarity at its highest is not in simplification, but in **Anticipatory Resonance**, that rare, sacred ability to sense what must come next, not through control, but through attunement.

The Guardians of Generality: Exhausted by the Ideal

Now consider the **Guardians of Generality**, the 80% whose lives can be characterized not as lacking in effort, but more frequently as driven by constant fatigue in trying to keep up with the continually retreating goal of perfection. For them, "getting it right" becomes synonymous with "being enough." The pressure to arrive, and to finally hit that imagined point of wholeness, can be suffocating. And when they inevitably fall short (as we all do), they are told to chase harder, to manifest better, dream bigger, and to prove worthiness through endless striving.

They live in the echo of what we call **Bad Intel**, misinformation that equates external validation with inner truth. They chase the carrot, but the carrot keeps moving. And in that loop, confidence is replaced by anxiety, and ambition becomes injury-prone. They are not failing; they are being misled. They are not lazy. they are coded to chase a version of perfection that does not actually exist. And here is the turning point, when they finally begin to understand that **perfection is not a goal, but a garden**, everything changes. A garden is not built in a day. It is nurtured, watered, and tended. It grows not through force, but through care. This is the lesson of **Organic Foundation** that growth, when aligned with rhythm, becomes sustainable.

Worthiness as Compass, Not Reward

In the middle of this dichotomy stands the **Conscious Integrator**, the Translator, those who understand that the issue is not perfection itself, but the issue is how we define and pursue it. To them, **worthiness is not something to be earned**, but something to be remembered. It is not a carrot bound to achievement, but an internal compass that guides the act of becoming. This evolution, from external pursuit to internal alignment, is nothing short of radical. It changes perfection from a noun into a verb. It transforms failure from a flaw into feedback. And it reframes success not as superiority, but as synchronicity.

The Integrator is not here to declare which side is right. They are here to weave the two together, gently, consistently, without shame. They show the Guardian how rhythm creates reliability. They remind the Architect that elegance without accessibility is not coherence. They teach us all that Integrated Perfection is not a compromise, but it is the highest fidelity we can offer to life

Dynamic Integration: Perfection in Motion

What makes **Integrated Perfection** different from idealism is that it is not about reaching a flawless state. It is about *moving with presence through the unfolding*. Like a jazz musician responding to the band, or a sculptor carving from what the stone reveals, it is a living, relational form of intelligence.

And here, **Faith as the Fruit of Formed Practice** emerges. Not blind faith, but proved trust. The sort that creates not through a doctrine, but through a pattern. Through the practice of showing up in rhythm, honoring the signals, and weaving with care. This is the **Synaptic Dance** at its best, when precision meets compassion, when structure meets surrender, and when knowledge no longer divides, but directs.

Legacy and Praxis

The work of the Integrator becomes one of **Propagation of Praxis**, the ongoing practice of living truth through form. Not theorizing about it. Not preaching it. But forming it, daily, in how we speak, move, build, and relate. They do not ask for applause. They ask for coherence. They do not leave behind legacies of domination or control, but rather the seeds of **Worthy Progress**. Their true impact does not always appear immediately, but it is felt deeply, within the systems that soften, in individuals who finally find their breath, and in environments where becoming feels safe again.

And in that environment, perfection is no longer feared or worshipped. It is *lived*. Not as a flawless product, but as a fluid, evolving process of weaving truth into time.

Final Reflection: Rewriting the Code

The glitch was never the bug; it was always the flag.

The rigid ideas, the false dichotomy, the unconscious and endless chase for the carrot, these were never failures. They were invitations. Warnings that the old story of perfection was never ours to begin with. And now, we have a chance to write a new one.

A story where the **Architects refine**, the **Guardians rise with rhythm**, and the **Integrators guide the weave**. A story where **perfection is not purity**, but alignment. Not an arrival, but an artistry. And the true compass? It was never the carrot. It was worthiness, felt within, pointing quietly home.

"True perfection is not the cleanest line. It is the truest one. The one drawn with care, in motion, in presence, in love."

Chapter 9

The Lexicon of Integration: Crafting the Language of Spectrum and Process

Language is not only a means of communication; it is what defines the reality we actually live. Words contain our world, establish our relationships, and give us a path to deal with life itself. The construction of a new lexicon, or creating a new way of being, is in fact the embodiment of the totality of complexity and interrelatedness of life."

The Grand Disconnect: The Need for a New Language

We live in an age where we are surrounded by information. Every day, we receive more data, more facts, more insights than ever before. It looks like we should be more in touch, be more in sync, more aware, more unified. And yet, the opposite is true. Despite all the knowledge we have at our fingertips, we are more fragmented, more disconnected than ever before. The problem isn't that we lack knowledge. The issue is how we are using it, or rather, how we are not using it in a way that connects us. Something is missing there: integration. We have all the pieces, but we are not putting them together. We have data, we have insights, but they are scattered, and it is due to our inherent distraction caused by the way we talk.

The language we have inherited does not reflect the complexity of life. Instead, it simplifies things into neat categories that are easy to understand, good and bad, right and wrong, and true and false. Although this simplification fulfills its goal, it also reduces our capacity to view the world as it actually is, dynamic, intertwined, and diverse. It locks us in old structures that no longer fit the reality we are living in.

Language: The Divide to Connection

The **Grand Disconnect** is not just a case of missing a piece of information; it is about the way we present that information. The language we use keeps us from seeing the bigger picture. It is built for efficiency, yes, but not for understanding. This is because no matter how hard or sincerely you try, it is impossible to connect with other people without the proper language, or to have a full picture of our experiences, to incorporate the knowledge we possess into something that matters.

For the **Architects of Nuance**, the few who see through this barrier, the problem with language is evident everywhere. Words are not just a means of communication to them. Words shape our reality. But the current lexicon, with all its oversimplifications and rigid boundaries, cannot reflect the full spectrum of our existence. It reduces our complexity and divides us from each other and from ourselves. The answer is simple, though not easy: We need a new lexicon. This is not a language of compartmentalized life, a language that holds to the one thing and lets the other go, a language that makes no claims on life, that does not reduce and simplify, a language that does not estrange, nor immerse, nor subsume. But this Lexicon of Integration would not be an instrument, but the means of overcoming the gap. A new language for a new way of seeing the world.

The Architects of Nuance and Their Quest for Precision

To the Architects of Nuance, those 20% who are naturally sensitized to life complexities, the barrage of language is therefore both a problem and a weapon for them. They know that the current language often fails them. It does not have the capability of understanding the complexity of their thoughts and the lives and experiences, as well as the world around them. So, they look for something deeper, something that is not constrained by rigid definitions or binary thinking.

To them, language does not lie in simplifying things; instead, it lies in the ability to state things as they really are, contradictory, ambiguous, and manifold. They do not seek language that fits in the old pattern of rules; they are looking for language that adapts to the complexity of reality. The **Lexicon of Integration** is not merely a question of inventing new words; it is about rethinking how we use the words we already have.

The Four Pillars of the Lexicon

In shaping this Lexicon of Integration, we should assume four fundamental principles.

1. The Language of Denial and Undoing

This does not mean saying no; it is a matter of breaking things down. It is the language of release, of doubt, of questioning the assumptions, and of making space and time to think differently. By rejecting the old conceptions and notions, we create room to see, understand, and interpret properly. we make space for clarity and understanding. It is the language of deconstruction, but with the purpose of rebuilding something better.

2. The Language of Process and Emergence (without Origin)

Life is always changing. It is not about a fixed point of origin; it is about a continual process of becoming. This language reflects the fluidity of existence, the changeability of being, the idea that everything is in a state of motion, constantly changing. It acknowledges that the world does not remain the same, nor can our language remain so. It is a growth language rather than a language of completion.

3. The Language of Paradox and Contradiction

This is where things get messy and beautiful. The world is full of contradictions. And instead of shying away from them, this language embraces them. It understands that life is not just black and white. It is full of shades, and sometimes the answers lie not in one extreme or the other, but in the space between. The language is true in many ways, providing us with the possibility to regard this world in all its complexity.

4. The Language of Experience and Effect (without Cause)

This is a language of life, of sensation, of personality. It pays respect to the fact that life is not really as straightforward as cause and effect. There are times that things are that way, and that is all. And rather than attempting to correlate each outcome with a certain cause, such language is concerned with consequences--how experiences ripple on and form us. It is a language of harmony, of instinct, of understanding without having to interpret everything.

The Guardians of Generality and Their Struggle with Language

To the **Guardians of Generality**, 80 percent of the people who live within established systems, language is a burden and a comfort at the same time. It guides them around the world, but it also frequently seems restrictive. They wish to have a language that would actually depict what they have been through and a language that would identify them to the world in a profound manner. However, what they end up with is simplified categories, fixed definitions, and hollow promises.

They have been taught to accept the language they have been given, but it often leaves them feeling unheard and misunderstood. So then, feeling frustrated is not their fault. It is an outgrowth of a system that has created their world and constrained their ability to participate more. They want a language that helps them interact with others, know themselves, and also determine their role in the world.

The Responsibility of Conscious Integrator

The Conscious Integrator is the one bridging this gap. They are not only interpreters of languages, but interpreters of realities. And they are the people who know all the tricky things about both the architects of Nuance and the guardians of Generality, and they assist in moving the two together. They invent a new vocabulary of language, which is not a simple stock of words but a collection of things that allow them to know about the world holistically in a more coherent manner.

It is they who will lead us towards a new way of speaking, a way of understanding, a mode of connection, and a mode of explanation. They work to develop a language, not a language about communication, but a language about change. The Lexicon of Integration is an instrument for healing, connection, and growth.

The Transformative Power of Language

Language is more than just conveying information; it is a way to create the world, it is not just an exchange of words but to understand the world's true essence. The **Lexicon of Integration** has the power to evolve everything. When we start talking the truth of the world in a way that mirrors the complexities of life, we use the words that embrace contradiction, complexity, and ambiguity, we create a new reality that is more real, more integrated, and more connected.

For the **Architects of Nuance**, this new lexicon will allow them to refine their intuitions and make their complex ideas in ways more ways to better understand. For the **Guardians of Generality**, it will give them the instruments to understand their world in a more meaningful way, to connect with others in a deeper way. And for the **Conscious Integrators**, it will be the key to bridging the divides and bringing coherence to the chaos.

Conclusion: A New Reality Through Words

The **Lexicon of Integration** is more than a new means of expression; it is a new way of seeing, of being, and of understanding. It is the instrument that is required to cure the Grand Disconnect, bringing us to a world where language is no longer a way to become divided, but rather has become a uniting power, knowledge should no longer be a way to become fragmented, instead, it is a tool that helps to unite, and truth should no longer be something that is hidden but on the contrary, it should come and reveal itself.

Through this new language, we create the world we are in. And by doing so we form ourselves. This is the strength of words; not descriptive, but creative. This is the Lexicon of Integration, the language of the new world, a world in which complexity is welcomed, connection is fostered, and truth is lived

"A new lexicon doesn't just change how we speak; it changes how we live."

Chapter 10

The Deliberate Obscuration: Weeding Out Intentional Deception

"Deception thrives where truth is obscured, but the clarity to see through it is the power to reclaim what was always ours."

In every system, whether it is social, political, or economic, we find that there is a subtle force, something which not only serves to keep ignorance in darkness, but does this by falsehood. This is where the **Deliberate Obscuration** begins. It is not the result of a simple error, not a matter of forgotten context or accidental misunderstanding; this is something far more insidious. It is the purposeful concealment of truth. A strategic manipulation of perception that sows falsehoods into the very narratives that define how we understand the world.

This **Obscuration** is not accidental; it is a deliberate manipulation, a distortion set up to define the limits, to frame an awareness, and, finally, to limit Action Potential. It is done to keep people blinded; they do not want people to live and know how powerful they can be. It is not just one little slip, unintentional, of judgment; it is a systemic behavioral practice, it is within the way in which we are taught to think, conditioned into viewing the world.

To the Architects of Nuance, the group that represents the 20 percent who look beyond the surface to discover more, that willful deceit is their form of epistemological warfare. It is not just a lie alone, but it is a systematic twisting of reality. The Architects recognize that words cannot be innocent; they are used intentionally. The weaponized use of the word is the apparently benign "The". It is an impossibility of an initial point, a forced singularity that forbids the fluidity and complexity of things. By shaping narratives around these rigid structures, we lose sight of the **authentic spectrum of reality**. This is the heart of **The Engineered Divide**, where subtle linguistic manipulations perpetuate the **Deliberate Rot** that feeds systemic misunderstanding.

This **Bad Intel** is not about confusion; it is about control. It is about shaping thought in such a way that we cannot access the full range of possibilities available to us. It silences **humility** and ensures that humanity remains unaware of its true **Action Potential**. This is not a glitch; it is a design. It is a closed loop that keeps people in the dark, locked in patterns of misunderstanding and unconscious compliance.

The Architects of Nuance: Seeing Through the Veil

For the **Architects of Nuance**, the 20% who are able to see the cracks in our understanding, this deliberate deception is a **breach of ontological truth**. They are aware of how anything that is not the truth, even when it is a little bit, is the root of corruption of knowledge. These are people who know the language of Obscuration, how the most minute intentional omission may distort a whole story. The world does not appear to them as simple. It is disjointed, sophisticated, complex, and full of contradictions that deserve to be embraced, not hidden.

The Architects never simply take what they are given-they question it. They deconstruct. They dismantle the false narratives that keep society in a state of unconsciousness. They identify the violation in a clear and objective way and illuminate the lies that control our mental faculties. They are broke-backed in their efforts to reinstate **Anticipatory Resonance**, the capacity to know and feel what is to occur before it does-not by sight prediction but by organic knowledge of situation and by tone.

And it is not only intellectual work; this is ethical work. It's the pursuit of precision, the action of defending truth against the erosion caused by manufactured realities. They do not merely concentrate on the revelation of hidden truths, but strive to make the said truths occupy their essence in the common consciousness. So, by doing so, they aid in restoring integrity to our conceptions, which allows the **Thirst Monster** of misguided ambition not to mislead us.

The Guardians of Generality: Trapped in the Web of Deception

For the **Guardians of Generality**, the 80% of society that operates within well-established structures, intentional deception shows up as something much subtler. They experience it not as a direct lie, but as a persistent feeling that they are "kept in the dark," fed fragmented pieces of information that don't seem to add up. It is the experience of being tricked, of not being given the whole picture. And worse, it is the deep frustration of seeing miracle solutions presented that promise immediate transformation but never deliver.

The deception does not always seem like a lie; it is often a carefully crafted confusion. It is a cycle of receiving bits of information that trigger automatic biases, creating a cognitive loop that makes people believe they are being productive, but in reality, they are just repeating the same ineffective patterns. The expectation to the Guardians is achieved through conditioning, and as such, the Guardians cannot free themselves of the narratives that have been established when they are born.

The real issue for the Guardians is the way they are fed unproductive solutions. hey are admonished to rush, to pursue success, not to consider the slow, methodical procedure by which real change is always brought to pass. Instead, they are socialized to jump over patience, to seek instant gratification, which ultimately undermines any sustainable progress. The Bad Intel they consume keeps them locked in a closed loop, and they just keep working and never get the deeper 'meaning' they are so badly seeking

The Conscious Integrator: Naming the Breach

For the **Conscious Integrator**, the Translator of truth, this represents the hardest part of their work. Their role is clear: weeding out intentional deceptions. Their job is to name the breach and expose the mechanisms behind the deception with unwavering clarity. They are tasked with guiding others through this cognitive subversion, helping them break free from the closed loops created by Bad Intel.

This is where their biggest strength is. They do not merely relay the insights of the Architects; they put them in actionable terms that the Guardians can follow. Through them, they make people realize that they have been manipulated, have been deprived of their real Action Potential. In their thought positioning resonance, or simply pausing and reflecting, they assist other human beings to reorient beyond the invested assumptions and diminishing returns so as to open up to the opportunity to make new and more conscious decisions in their lives.

This is a practical exercise of making sophisticated knowledge into simple practice. It is the Integrators who are mediating between the Architects and the Guardians so that knowledge does not disappear in the intellectual scale; it needs to be transformed into material to be accessible and to be useful to all. They promote democratic complexity, where diverse perspectives are not only tolerated but embraced as sources of collective greatness in the journey toward an integrated future.

Conclusion: Unleashing True Action Potential

The Deliberate Obscuration is not only an abstract problem; it is systematic, and it is one that impacts all persons. From the **Architects of Nuance** to the **Guardians of Generality**, we are all vulnerable to the effects of intentional deception. Yet through the efforts of the Conscious Integrators, we can recapture the truth. We can escape the Engineered Divide and begin to progress towards a reality based on authentic growth and sustainable change.

By weeding out intentional deceptions, by naming the breach and exposing the lies, we unlock our true Action Potential. And this is the beginning of an integrated reality, a reality where truth reigns, knowledge can no longer be used as a means of control, but as a means of liberation, and where the world is no longer split apart by lies but united by clarity and precision and the common search for Integrated Perfection.

"In the face of deception, clarity is the first step to reclaiming our true potential. Only through exposing the falsehoods can we break free and unite in the pursuit of truth and integrated growth."

Chapter 11

The Fractured Mirror: Deconstructing Disrespect and Its Rejection for All

"When the mirror is cracked, the reflection deceives not only the eye, but the soul that trusts it."

The Unfolding Error does not only work in the realm of personal choice. When paired with the Sunk Cost Fallacy, it becomes a trap large enough to hold entire civilizations. Once a people have invested centuries into a story, defended it, built laws on it, and taught children to revere it, the cost of questioning that story feels almost unbearable. This is not just a habit; it is characteristic bound into the cement of identity.

And here, in the heaviness of that cement, we get the Fractured Mirror. This mirror does not reflect glass, but a story. It reflects what we have been told is our truest image, yet the reflection is bent and hairline-cracked, altering the face we think we see. Over generations, those cracks have been mistaken for natural features. We have forgotten there was ever another shape. One of the deepest fractures runs through the patriarchal foundations of ancient texts such as *the Bible*. These are not inoffensive relics of the past. They are man-made structures, with the divine stamp of approval, which exalt one group of the population and, at the same time, humiliate the other in silence. And in the process, they diminish the full humanity of both. The illusion of superiority is, in truth, a slow erosion, hollowing out the very capacities it claims to protect.

What may look like a cultural oversight is instead a multi-generational wound; a deliberate misalignment that distorts the essence of Integrated Perfection. It seeds the Engineered Divide, ensuring Wholism remains elusive. At its core is *Bad Intel*: a false coding woven so deeply into our creation myths that humility itself is silenced, and our shared *Action Potential* is quietly strangled before it can emerge.

The Architects of Nuance: the ones who see the fracture in the design

For the discerning 20%, the flaw is unmistakable. They see that "male headship" creation myths are not harmless traditions but ontological locks, fixed Beginnings that rot diversity at the root. These are more than role-assigning myths, since they also render them legislative prescriptions, making The Curse of the Unconscious part of the culture operating system. In this design, domination is mistaken for greatness, obedience for virtue, and questioning for betrayal. The result is an Invisible Box; meticulously constructed, rigid in its boundaries, that limits the holistic capacity and authentic expression of everyone inside it.

The Architects know this is no accident. It is the product of deliberate authorship: a historical breach that severed humanity from its Organic Reference and Embodied Laws. They recognize it as a core unfolding error, the origin of The Deliberate Rot, which keeps Anticipatory Resonance from ever coming into being.

The Guardians of Generality: the ones who live within the fracture

For the other 80%, the wound is harder to name. It shows up as "unspoken rules" about gender, or the quiet exhaustion of living in a role that never quite fits. Their desire and gifts are stifled by expectations so old they feel like the air itself. Here, the sunk cost is not only personal, but it is collective. To challenge it feels like losing a piece of oneself, even when that piece was never truly theirs. The result is endless cycles of argument, "offending each other" over surface disputes, while the deeper wound goes untouched.

Their Compliant Consciousness struggles to see the sleight of hand. They are fed the magic trick of non-informing data; information that looks like truth but is structured to prevent real understanding. This keeps them in a fabricated reality of narrow roles and chronic disease. Without humility to challenge these *Bad Intel* stories, their *Response Ability* remains asleep, and with it, their true *Action Potential.*

The Conscious Integrator / Translator: the ones who repair the mirror

For those rare individuals who stand between the two, the fracture is not something to observe; it is something to heal. Their task is to *name the breach* with both clarity and compassion, to practice *Assessment as Honesty* even when it unsettles or offends. Their job is a type of *Nobel Peace Prize function:* translating profound systemic analysis into terms that everyday lives can engage with.

They model athletic humility, the capacity to admit that the story you have built upon was flawed, and the courage to pivot without shame. They know that sharing of power, of roles, of vulnerability, is not loss but expansion. They place *Acceptance* at the center, turning it into an axis for true democratic complexity. They initiate the Synaptic Dance that reconnects us to the Organic Foundation, that buried memory of what authentic human connection feels like.

For them, Communication is God, not as dogma, but as a living truth: the act of speaking and listening with integrity is the force capable of healing the deepest divides. And there, in that restoration, is grace, growth, and the forward pull toward the Syntropic Future, a future in which wholeness is not an illusion but a lived experience.

"To reject the fractured mirror is not to abandon tradition. It is to abandon the lie dressed as truth. And when we finally see ourselves, and each other, without distortion, the work of mending becomes not just possible, but inevitable."

Chapter 12
The Uncrossable Obstacles: Nailed by Conditioning

"The strongest walls are not built of stone, but of the stories, we are told we cannot question."

The architects of intentional deception understood something most people never stop to consider: If you want to control the future, you must first own the past. And if you intend to own the past, you must make the path to reimagining it appear impossible to cross.

These are the uncrossable obstacles, not simple guideposts, but engineered barriers. They are made so accurately that they never instruct but restrain; never defend but shackle. They are crafted with precision, designed not to enlighten but to confine; not to protect, but to bind. Sometimes the binding is metaphorical, locking the human spirit inside inherited thought-forms. Sometimes, across history, it has been literal, enforced through laws, systems, and visible chains. In both cases, the result is the same: we are kept inside a fabricated reality with no safe exit.

This is one of the master mechanisms of the Engineered Divide: to install structures so fixed and so culturally sacred that they appear unassailable. It is the way The Deliberate Rot is maintained; Bad Intel is entrenched in the code of consciousness. These barriers silence humility before it can awaken, cutting us off from our true Action Potential.

The Architects of Nuance, the ones who see the mechanics of the wall

For the discerning 20%, these obstacles are not random misfortunes. They are **acts of epistemological engineering**, the intentional shaping of knowledge to limit what can be imagined. The Architects notice how even language is weaponized. The simple use of "*the*," a word that seems harmless, is deployed to confer singular authority: *The* truth, *The* way, *The* beginning. Each use tightens the lock. Miracles are reframed as distant events granted by something outside ourselves, instead of emergent results of discipline, process, and collective skill.

They see how Binary Divides, light/dark, male/female, chosen/rejected, are forged to create fractures within fractures. Layer upon layer, these become the invisible ribs of the Invisible Box, structures that block Anticipatory Resonance and quietly suffocate imagination before it can grow wild. The unfooled eye of the Architect can trace these threads back to their origin: the unfolding error that keeps humanity tethered to illusions. They know the obstacle is not the wall itself, but the conditioning that convinces people the wall is the edge of the world.

The Guardians of Generality: the ones living inside the wall

For the other 80%, these obstacles are experienced as unquestioned truths, rules so embedded in daily life that they feel like nature itself. They are presented in the form of strict customs, undisputed authorities, and social expectations so imminent that resistance feels almost sacrilegious. They are, in a sense, *nailed* to these frameworks, held in place by conditioning so complete that its origins have vanished from memory. In this Curse of the Unconscious, beliefs are followed automatically, without recognition of the original context. Thinking of breaking these barriers already provokes anxiety, fear, or shame.

The weight of sunk cost makes it worse. A lifetime invested in a set of beliefs builds a fierce loyalty to them, even when they limit the believer's own life. The result is a kind of spiritual claustrophobia: frustration without a name, conflict without resolution. They keep searching for *miracles*; quick, external interventions, rather than building the patient process that true transformation requires. Without humility for self-assessment, the Bad Intel remains unchallenged, their Response Ability is stunted, and their Action Potential is left dormant. They go over and over the same plot in their heads, not knowing that not everything is on the horizon.

The Conscious Integrator / Translator: the ones who unfasten the nails

For the rare few who straddle both worlds, these uncrossable obstacles are not merely problems; they are prime targets for conscious reclamation. It is the core work of their Nobel practice: not only to label the walls, but to provide a key to the back gate. They begin with the Sacred Pause, that intentional stillness where the reflex to react is suspended long enough to *see* the structure of the barrier itself. In that pause, fear loosens. Space opens. Truth can be examined without the distortions of urgency or defensiveness. Here, they model athletic humility, the courage to admit when we have been misled, and the willingness to pivot without self-condemnation. They remind us that honesty is not a verdict, but a process.

Their work is to "un-mail" minds, to unfasten the conditioning nails, piece by piece, revealing that many of the obstacles were never as solid as they seemed. In doing so, they open the *Portal* to genuine democratic complexity and the kind of growth that emerges, naturally and unstoppably, when freedom is no longer theoretical. In their vision, Faith is not blind belief. It is *the fruit of formed practice*; the lived confidence that comes from nurturing real capacity. And in that practice, Integrated Perfection is not something that stays an ideal, but is something moving, growing, and changing.

Their humility is the quiet spark that ignites liberation; the spark that turns "impossible" into "already happening." In that light, the walls melt, the obstacles become transparent, and the human spirit steps forward, without the chains of the past, into the Syntropic Future.

Conclusion: Seeing the Gate in the Wall

The greatest trick of the uncrossable obstacle is not its strength, but its disguise. It persuades us that rebellion is futile, that the wall is the edge, that the horizon is the boundary. For the Architects, this means dismantling the design. For the Guardians, it begins with recognizing the discomfort as a sign, not a flaw. For the Conscious Integrator, it is opening the door wide enough for others to see the truth for themselves.

When we see these barriers as constructed illusions, intentional shaping of thought to enclose the human spirit, their strength dissolves. What once looked like solid stone reveals itself as paper and ink. To step beyond them is not to abandon the safety of what we have known. It is to reclaim the safety we were promised but never given. It is to see that the "uncrossable" was only ever a word, and that words can be redefined. And once the wall is breached, there is no going back. The conditioning loses its hold. The mind, un-nailed, moves toward its full Action Potential, and humanity, piece by piece, begins to remember how far it was always meant to go.

"The moment the wall is seen for what it is, the horizon changes, and the question is no longer whether we can cross, but how far we are willing to go."

Chapter 13

The Unspeakable Frontier: Crafting Language for the "Before the Before"

"The surest way to keep a mind from crossing the frontier is to erase the map to it — and convince it the land was never there."

The most dangerous deception is not a false story. It is the quiet, practically imperceptible process of removing the ability in us to envision more than the story told to us. The Source, whether framed as *The Beginning* or *The Truth*, becomes a kind of conceptual circuit breaker. By declaring a definite beginning or a final ending that it erases silently the potentiality for anything preceding that beginning or following that ending. It tells us that the unseen hill cannot be climbed because it does not exist.

This is more than a limit on information; it is a limit on thought itself. A type of *conceptual prohibition* that keeps awareness bound within given limits. It reinforces the walls of the Invisible Box, reduces the margins of possibility, and suppresses the very Action Potential on which our human nature is built. In the architecture of control, this is one of the purest mechanisms of the Engineered Divide; a quiet but potent element of The Deliberate Rot. It is Bad Intel disguised as absolute truth, coding consciousness so deeply that humility and expansion cannot take root.

The Architects of Nuance: the ones who cross the edge

For the discerning 20%, this is the ultimate **Curse of the Unconscious,** not just believing the wrong thing, but losing the ability to even *conceive* of the alternative. It is ontological amnesia: the quiet forgetting that there could be a "before the before," or a reality wider than the official frame.

They view how blind acceptance of predetermined (preconceived) Beginnings ties the Compliant Consciousness down to limited mental systems. They can trace the stitching of the box: the single, sanctioned origin; the neatly packaged truth; the linguistic patterns that make the cage invisible.

To work at the Unspeakable Frontier demands a rare kind of courage, an *epistemological courage*, to breach the unmarked boundaries, to allow thought to wander into the "impossible," and to reclaim the capacity for radical inquiry. Their craft is a Synaptic Dance that moves beyond habitual thinking, seeking to restore Anticipatory Resonance by reweaving the Organic Reference that has been cut away. They know the cost of staying inside the sanctioned perimeter, and the cost of leaving it, but they step beyond anyway.

The Guardians of Generality: the ones living in the shadow of the wall

For the 80%, this limitation feels less like theft and more like comfort. It shows up as a readiness to accept "The Beginning" without asking what came before, or to accept "The Truth" without wondering what lies beyond it. These boundaries are rarely questioned because they are rarely visible; they arrive wrapped in the language of normalcy. Without knowing it, they inherit a worldview where certain questions are filed under *unknowable* or *irrelevant*. And in so doing, they lose all the productive discomfort associated with real growth. The loneliness of misunderstanding lingers, not as a sharp wound, but as a dull ache that never quite heals.

Confined by the very language they use, they are more easily swayed by non-informing data, facts that seem conclusive but keep

70

thought safely inside the box. At some point, the sunk cost of their investment in these fixed positions becomes increasingly burdensome. Without humility to challenge their own limits, the *Bad Intel* remains their operating system, their *Response Ability* remains dormant, and their true *Action Potential* never takes form.

The Conscious Integrator / Translator: the ones who give the map back

For the rare few who choose to work at the edge, the *Unspeakable Frontier* is not just an abstract concept; it is their terrain. Their work is the deliberate, patient reclamation of the collective imagination. They do this by crafting the *Lexicon of Integration*, a language that can reach beyond the sanctioned frame and speak to the "before the before" without collapsing into dogma. They use the *Unveiling Tongue* with precision:

- **The Language of Negation and Un-doing;** dissolving the false without rushing to fill the gap.
- **The Language of Process and Emergence;** speaking of change without an imposed origin.
- **The Language of Paradox and Contradiction;** allowing truths to coexist without flattening them into one.
- **The Language of Experience and Effect without Cause;** honoring what is real without forcing it into a single narrative.

By making this language accessible, they *un-mail* the collective mind, removing the conditioning nails one by one, and open the door to *Syntropic Resonance*, the natural movement toward greater order and emergent potential. In their vision, *Faith* is not blind allegiance to a fixed beginning. It is *the fruit of formed practice;* a trust built by direct experience and disciplined engagement. Within this kind of space, Integrated Perfection does not become a destination, but a dynamic process where we live. It is at their humility that they cross, and it is through their craftsmanship that they bridge.

Conclusion: Beyond the Named Horizon

The Unspeakable Frontier will never be represented on a map made by people with a fear of it. To approach it is to refuse the comfort of the single story, to accept that truth expands faster than language can contain it. For the Architects, this means pressing past the perimeter until the false edges dissolve. In the case of the Guardians, it starts with only a simple courage: asking the question the map tells them not to ask.

For the Conscious Integrator, it is the lifelong labor of giving others not the answer, but the compass. And once a mind has glimpsed the "before the before," no boundary can fully hold it again. The box becomes transparent. The Bad Intel loses its grip. And the human spirit, unbound by the false horizon, begins the work of imagining what was once unspeakable into being.

"Once the mind has glimpsed the land before the beginning, no map can contain it, and no wall can hold it."

Chapter 14

The Unveiling Tongue: Language Re-Forged to Reveal What It Hid

"Language is both the window and the wall, and for too long, we have mistaken the frame for the view."

The most dangerous deception is not always the lie we are told; it is the limits we have stopped noticing. They slip in quietly, they are given to us without our questioning, and we have inherited them without a murmur of protest; and they are stitched into the very language and thought we use every day.

Language, our oldest instrument of connection, has also, over centuries, become a quiet architect of confinement. Words, born from specific beginnings and shaped for particular purposes, have built an Invisible Box around the reach of our collective imagination. This is the paradox of *"crafting language to reveal what language once concealed."* The same system we rely on to make sense of reality can also frame the limits of this existence, which means that we will hardly go outside the lines of this system

When we fail to question the structures of our language, the familiar patterns of syntax and the inherited meanings beneath them, they become quiet barriers. These barriers do not just limit what we can say; they quietly restrict what we can think. And in that narrowing, the spark of Anticipatory Resonance is smothered before it has a chance to arise and take shape. They feed the Grand Disconnect and preserve The Deliberate Rot. This unconscious coding, Bad Intel at the level of language itself, stifles humility and constricts humanity's true Action Potential.

The Architects of Nuance: the ones who work at the foundation of meaning

For the discerning 20%, the concealment built into language is more than a flaw; it is an irony at the core of human knowing. They see the layered fracture in cognition caused by linguistic habits so deeply ingrained that we no longer hear them. They hear the quiet authority in the definite article *"The"*: *The* truth. *The* way. *The* beginning. They see how it quietly seals thought within a single lane. They observe that language settles back into established reference marks, cementing assumptions before thought even begins.

Their work is part archaeology, part alchemy. They dig into the strata of words to recover lost context, unmask intentional distortions, and re-forge the materials of communication so that meaning carries its full, untwisted weight. In this way, they start breaking the Curse of the Unconscious, changing it into the intentional course toward accuracy and strength. This is the *unfooled eye* applied to the very medium of human thought. It is how they begin to restore the *Embodied Law* of clear articulation, and how they start to mend the *Severed Genesis* caused by the *Erasure of Organic Reference*. In their hands, language stops being a cage and becomes a crafted vessel, capable of carrying truth intact into the *Syntropic Future*.

The Guardians of Generality: the ones who feel the gap but cannot name it

For the 80%, the problem is felt rather than dissected. They know the frustration of words that "fall short," that flatten lived experience into something smaller, or that force them into rigid *either/or* choices that deny their complexity. When language fails, it breeds a subtle loneliness, the kind that comes from knowing what you mean but having no way to truly say it. Every day speech, automatic and inherited, keeps them *mailed by conditioning*. The unspoken assumptions buried in ordinary talk slip past their awareness, reinforcing the Engineered Divide without their consent.

This makes them easy prey for *non-informing data,* statements that feel authoritative but do nothing to illuminate. In a world that is full of noise, they crave language that will root them down, make them fear less, and show their reality with integrity. They want words that work, that give them anchors in a shifting landscape, that guide them toward functional knowledge and allow them to engage their *Response Ability* with confidence. But without humility to question the structures they have inherited, **Bad Intel** remains embedded in their communication. As a result, all this leads to a circle of misunderstanding breeding frustration, frustration breeding inaction, and the possibility of more understanding bound behind the very words they rely on.

The Conscious Integrator / Translator: The ones who give language back its wholeness

For the rare few working between these two worlds, the challenge is not just to notice language's limits, it is to reshape it so it can hold more truth. This is their Nobel function: to craft the Lexicon of Integration, a living language designed to connect realities and heal fractures rather than widen them.

They wield the **Unveiling Tongue** with intent, using it to break patterns and invite new ways of thinking:

- **The Language of Negation and Un-Doing,** clearing away what is false without rushing to fill the gap.
- **The Language of Process and Emergence (without Origin);** describing growth without binding it to a single start.

- **The Language of Paradox and Contradiction;** holding complexity without flattening it into certainty.
- **The Language of Experience and Effect (without Cause);** honoring what is felt and observed without forcing it into a predetermined chain.

This is what makes them translators of the unconscious because this language is made available and familiar. The reason is that they craft speech that brings people together instead of letting them tear apart, that makes democratic phenomena possible instead of letting them be impossible, that renders communication an act of synthesis instead of a process of fragmentation. Each word is, in its vision, a *Legacy Seed Sown with Integrity,* carrying within it the potential for clarity, trust, and shared reality. In this case, Faith is not an abstract belief, but *the fruit of formed practice,* which has been created by a disciplined expression and careful listening. cultivated through disciplined expression and intentional listening.

They live the truth that **"Communication is God,"** not as a slogan, but as a living act that shapes reality itself. Word by word, they transform confusion into coherence, fragmentation into *Wholism,* and language into a generative power source for collective greatness.

Conclusion: Speaking Beyond the Frame

The first step to reclaiming language is to notice its frame, to realize that the words we inherited are not the whole of what can be said. The Unveiling Tongue does more than refine speech; it rewrites the boundaries of thought.

For the Architects, this is the patient reconstruction of meaning from its foundation. For the Guardians, it begins with recognizing the discomfort of being misunderstood as a clue to expand their vocabulary of truth. For the Conscious Integrator, it is the ongoing craft of building a lexicon that not only describes reality but also enlarges it.

When language is freed from the walls it built, the horizon of meaning extends, and for the first time, we begin to speak what was once unthinkable.

Chapter 15

The Deliberate Rot: Weaponizing Singularity to Destroy Diversity

"When truth is narrowed to a single voice, the silence that follows is not peace, it is erasure."

There are deceptions so small that they slip past unnoticed: misstatements, misunderstandings, errors of perception. But then there are others. They do not emerge by accident, nor from the flaws of language, nor the natural limits of human comprehension, but they are planted with precision. They are nurtured like precious plants, but the reward is no longer truth but domination. At the heart of this more dangerous category lies a particular strategy, the weaponization of singularity. This is not merely the telling of a false tale, but intentionally squeezing reality into a narrow, single, rigid frame, one that can exclude, erase, and ultimately destroy the various perspectives that give human understanding its depth. It is the tightening of the aperture until only one line of sight remains, and all others are cast into shadow.

Once singularity is used as a weapon, diversity is not just ignored, but it is systematically broken apart. Every lie embedded in the core stories has a goal: to limit what people notice, influence how they understand it, and decrease their ability to act. This is not a passive decay but a deliberate rot, a designed pathology that thrives on uniformity, ensuring that only the engineered story survives.

The Architects: Reading the Pattern of the Cage

For the few who can see it, the Architects of Nuance, the structure is unmistakable. They are the 20% who refuse to avert their gaze when they notice the edges do not align. Their attention is not distracted by the surface gloss; they read the blueprint beneath. They understand that even the smallest elements, a single word like *"The"*, can serve as a lock on the mind. These seemingly harmless linguistic choices can frame entire realities, closing them off to the richness of alternatives. What appears as natural law is often nothing more than an engineered constant. The frame is built to conceal its scaffolding, so the design seems inevitable and unchangeable.

The Architects know that this concealment is not incidental. It is epistemological warfare, a breach of reality at its very foundation. Left unchallenged, it creates a loop of unconscious compliance: people act without questioning, repeat without examining, and live within boundaries they never saw being drawn. What the Architect does is, then, a form of rescue, not out of lack of knowledge, but from precision-engineered blindness.

The Guardians: Living Under the Weight of Fog

To the Guardians of Generality, the 80%, this distortion is rather sensed than observed. They can feel that something is "off," a contradiction between what they are told and what they experience, but without context, the feeling settles into background noise. They live with an ache for clarity that never quite resolves. And in the absence of a clear picture, the brain does what it must to survive: it fills the gaps with whatever is provided. Unfortunately, those gaps are often filled with "Bad Intel," data designed to mislead, to keep thought shallow, and to ensure that no sustained challenge to the singular narrative takes root.

This is why miracle solutions and easy answers are so seductive. They avoid the discomfort of deep analysis and, instead of facing it, they choose the quick gratification of certainty. However, these shortcuts are poison to genuine growth. They discourage patience, weaken the process, and diminish the value of complexity. The outcome is a passive mindset, cut off from the integrity of its own journey and unaware of the value of different viewpoints. In this way, the rot doesn't just misinform; it stunts. It keeps those who want change stuck in repetitive patterns. They are unwilling to let go of old investments, even if those investments are no longer productive.

The Integrators: Weeding the Garden of the Mind

For the Conscious Integrator, the translator between the Architects and the Guardians, this is the hardest terrain to navigate. Their role requires precision. They must identify and name the breach without tearing down the whole structure that people rely on for their daily lives. They cannot simply declare the truth; doing so too abruptly can fracture trust and deepen the divide. Instead, they need to work through the decay in shared reality, thread by thread, until what is left can stand without collapsing. This is why they turn the Architect's complex breakdowns into clear and easy-to-understand forms, delivering clarity without condescension. They realize that the most insidious lies are not spoken from podiums but quietly embedded in the language we speak daily. By naming these without turning the naming itself into a weapon, they keep the work from becoming another tool of division. They also understand the value of timing, of the "90 seconds of thought" that can shift a person's entire orientation. Sometimes, a single pause, a single reframing, or a new way of seeing can interrupt a chain of habitual thinking. The Integrator flourishes in these times, encouraging others to do the same until diversity is seen as the source of our strength rather than a threat.

The Cost of Letting the Rot Grow

The weaponization of singularity becomes self-reinforcing if it would be left unchecked. It suppresses humility, obliterates other routes, and formalises a mindset that views diversity as harmful. However, truth in real life is layered, evolutionary, dynamic, often contradictory in its specifics and peaceful in its essence. This rewrites the very thing of truth as something there is one of, and it stays that way. All that it takes to destroy it is the judgment of the Architect, the openness to question of the Guardian, and the ability of the Integrator to mend the divide. Otherwise, there is still this rot going on, not because it is mighty, but because it is maintained.

Beyond Singularity

Truth does not flourish in isolation. It grows in the interplay of perspectives, in the meeting of angles, in the respectful tension of differences. To weaponize singularity is to amputate that living process, to replace it with a brittle, lifeless replica. The work, then, is not only to expose the deliberate rot but to restore the soil it has poisoned.

It is only when diversity in all its different forms is permitted to breathe freely and without restriction, the total Action Potential can be fully achieved, and along with it the chance of an unmanufactured future.

The Deliberate Rot thrives in the fact that it has something to protect, and it is not the truth, but the fallacy that the truth is small enough to be covered. And the biggest threat to that illusion is not outrage or rebellion, but the quiet, inevitable dawning of the realization that the world was always bigger, wealthier, and interconnected than the frame suggested.

Which is why, in the shadow of every engineered fracture, something else waits. Not another false story, but the story before stories, the pull toward the whole. This is the horizon the Rot fears most. And it is here that our attention must turn next.

Chapter 16
Wholism: The Feared Horizon of Integrated Being

"The horizon is not the end of the road; it is where every road meets."

In the previous chapter, we uncovered the *Deliberate Rot*, a deliberate fracture designed to conceal truth and eliminate diversity. But knowing how a structure rots is not the same as knowing what a healthy structure looks like. If the Rot is the disease, *Wholism* is the health it fears most. And in a strange twist, that fear is exactly why the Rot exists.

Wholism, or Holism, is not a soft philosophical ornament. It is the *carrot and the horizon* in one: the living state of **Integrated Perfection**, where the scattered pieces of being align without losing their shape. But precisely because it erases the fractures on which control depends, Wholism is treated as a threat. The very method that could unite us is the one most fiercely resisted. This resistance is not random; it is cultivated, protected, and fed by the same *fabricated generalities* and *deceptive singularities* that hold the Engineered Divide in place. Fear becomes the gatekeeper, and "Bad Intel" becomes the lock.

The Architects of Nuance: Seeing Beyond the Fear

For the 20% who cannot look away, known as **Architects of Nuance,** Wholism a living truth, not a blur to be painted upon. They regard it as a dynamic unity or aggregate of some dynamic parts that exist within it, and each part still has its own uniqueness and actively contributes to the process of weaving relationships as integrated wholes. To them, Wholism is not a singular "The" imposed on reality, but a *co-arising* process, the manifestation of what some call the *before the before*.

But even here, fear has a foothold. Fear of losing the self in the whole. Fear of dissolving hard-won identity. Fear rooted in old competitive paradigms and fixed Beginnings. These anxieties/fears are intellectual barriers created and maintained to prevent the Unplannable Harvest, or the emergence of true integration; they are not personal flaws. If the underlying context is not seen, even the creative mind can get caught in an Invisible Box of its own presumptions. To the Architects, the realization that fear is the disease of an unconscious deception is the beginning of the reduction of this fear.

The Guardians of Generality: The Mirage of Division

For the **Guardians of Generality**, the 80%, Wholism frequently seems like an impending storm. The very thought of being absorbed into a larger whole threatens the comfort of familiar boundaries. Their minds gravitate toward binaries, neat categories, and clean lines. Integration, in contrast, looks messy, undefined, and even dangerous.

This fear is not instinctive; it is learned. It is the product of conditioning that whispers, *"Division is natural, unity is chaos."* And because the comfort of the known outweighs the discomfort of complexity, many remain trapped in loops of false conflict: constant debates over "right" and "wrong" that mask the deeper truth that both are fragments of a greater whole. Yet, the absence of Wholism is felt as lonely, isolating, and frustrating in ways words cannot describe. unable to exercise full Response Ability or realize authentic Action Potential.

The Conscious Integrator: Turning Fear into Connection

For the **Conscious Integrator / Translator**, Wholism is not only a goal, it is a duty. Their role is to dismantle the Rot and the Divide by making Wholism feel not like a loss, but a gain. They do this by *embodying* integration, modeling it so others can feel its truth rather than fear it. They understand that "real education is integration felt in the bones," a lived realism where the presence of others does not diminish you, but expands you. In this space, *sharing replaces the fear of loss.* Here, faith is not blind belief but the fruit of Formed Practice; the discipline of weaving complexity into coherence until the whole becomes as familiar as the part.

For them, Wholism is not an abstract reward at the end of the road; it is the road itself. By applying consistent, embodied protocols, they decode "Bad Intel" and restore the Organic Foundation of existence. In doing so, they turn fear into a tool. This is not for control, but for liberation. They release the collective Action Potential that a fractured world has kept hidden.

Wholism is not about erasing the self, but it is about recognizing that the self was never separate. To fear the whole is to fear the truth of your own belonging. And when that fear dissolves, what remains is not a horizon we approach, but one we finally step into, together.

Chapter 17

The Organic Foundation: Honesty in the Weave of Physiological Needs

"Before the spirit can rise, the body must be true."

Every great structure rests on a foundation. In human life, that foundation is not abstract, philosophical, or intellectual; it is physical. Before the mind can expand or the heart can open, the body must be in honest relationship with its own needs. Breath, water, nourishment, rest; these are not luxuries, nor simply "maintenance tasks." They are the Organic Foundation of being. Still, in our fractured world, even these simplest, fundamental truths are trapped within a tangle of lies and deception.

We live in a time where the essential is obscured. Physiological needs are rarely met in their pure, unadulterated form. They are filtered through a marketplace of quick fixes, manufactured cravings, and fabricated "solutions" that pull us further from our own rhythms. This dishonesty, whether it is intentional or unintentional, leads to a refusal to acknowledge what the body really needs. This refusal creates an early split in the fabric of life. It marks the beginning of the Grand Disconnect, long before we recognize its more complicated patterns.

This is not just a matter of bad habits. It is a deep systemic coding of "Bad Intel" into the very way we approach survival. We learn from a young age to react to our internal and external needs with noise, distraction, and a desperate search for quick satisfactions. This behavior is frequently driven by the tempting call of the Thirst

Monster. This creature comes from our unmet needs and societal pressures. It feeds on our cravings and keeps us stuck in a never-ending cycle of seeking approval from others and looking for instant relief. Each time we give in, we briefly ease our discomfort but make our sense of disconnection worse. This creates a pattern that drains our energy, distorts our perception, and suppresses the humility needed to return to center.

The Architects of Nuance: Seeing the Breach at the Root

For the **Architects of Nuance,** the 20% who have learned to look past surface narratives, the corruption at this level is glaring. They see how most systems for "servicing" basic needs are built on broken premises. Miracle diets that ignore the body's adaptation curve. Sleep "hacks" that cut rest into fragments. Supplements and stimulants that override fatigue rather than address it.

To them, these behaviors are not just wrong strategies or shallow coping methods. They see them as serious violations of the sacred bond between body and self. They realize that real healing and true restoration require patience, inner calm, and a respectful connection to one's natural rhythms. However, they also understand that this patience does not fit with the constant speed, distraction, and show put forth by consumer culture. This culture prioritizes instant satisfaction and shallow entertainment over real inner growth. They know that without returning to organic reference, a lived calibration to the body's real signals, integration will always be incomplete.

The Architect's unfooled eye catches the link between this dishonesty and the Deliberate Rot described earlier. If Wholism is feared, then distorting physiological truth is one of the surest ways to keep humanity disoriented. By scrambling the body's compass, the entire structure of conscious progression becomes unstable.

The Guardians of Generality: Living in the Disconnection

For the **Guardians of Generality**, the 80%, this dishonesty does not appear as a clear violation. It appears as a vague, persistent feeling of being "off." The signals are there, fatigue that does not lift, restlessness without cause, hunger that is not hunger, but the language to interpret them has been lost. In this state, life becomes a sequence of automatic responses to symptoms, rather than a conscious tending to needs. A sugar craving is answered with processed sweetness. Restlessness is drowned in entertainment. Dehydration hides under the mask of appetite. The natural connection between signal and fulfilment, along with the body's original context, is obscured by layers of convenience and habit.

This is a cycle of "offing ourselves" gradually; it goes beyond simple neglect. Chronic illness, low-grade exhaustion, and dis-ease become normalized. Quick fixes take the place of sustainable processes. And because the temporary relief feels easier than addressing the underlying cause, many people continue to be caught in a sunk cost loop, clinging to unsustainable practices that subtly undermine their Action Potential. The Guardians are easy targets for manufactured solutions that promise health but instead cause dependency in this state of compliant consciousness. Lack of humility when confronting primal truths makes sure that the "Bad Intel" re-encodes their bodies, trapping them in the fragmentation which they feel is irreversible.

The Conscious Integrator: Reclaiming the Foundation

For the **Conscious Integrator / Translator**, this is where the work begins. Their mission is not only to expose deception at the philosophical level, but to bring people back to their most elemental honesty. They know that if the body remains in deficit, all higher integration will collapse under strain. Their process is grounded in

Honesty as a Practice. Assessment is their first tool; teaching people to observe their own patterns without judgment, to track the gap between need and fulfillment. By exposing the sunk cost of unsustainable habits, they open the door to change rather than to shame people.

The Integrator understands that physiological needs are the root of Wholism. By restoring them, they restore the base layer of consciousness itself. They guide people toward organic progression, where small, consistent shifts: more water, unbroken rest, and unprocessed nourishment, rebuild the capacity for integrated living.

This re-grounding activates what they call the Neuro-Formulation Gateway, the point at which the nervous system, body, and mind come back into coherent conversation. From here, the Synaptic Dance transforms: no longer the frantic scramble of deficit, but the steady rhythm of Syntropic Resonance, energy that grows, builds, and sustains itself. When faith appears here, it is no longer blind. It is the fruit of formed practice, born of living proof that tending the foundation changes the whole structure.

The Organic Foundation is not just where we begin; it is where we live, every moment. Ignore it, and even the brightest vision will crumble. Honor it, and everything we build upon it will hold.

Chapter 18

The Alignment of Worthiness: Integrity as the Becoming of Truth

"Worth is not claimed, it is aligned."

The journey toward Wholism and Integrated Perfection is not a thought experiment. It is not something to be appreciated from a safe distance or understood only in theory. It is a rigorous, demanding, and life-changing process. At its core lies a decisive act: to surrender to truth, not once, but continually, through *honesty as a process*. And alongside that surrender is the equally vital choice to let *what is truly worthy* set the direction.

This is not abstract morality. It is a precise alignment; an unbroken thread between what we know, what we pursue, and how we act. That alignment is **Integrity**. It is the silent but fixed center from which all true integration can emerge, the Organic Foundation of true growth. Without it, even the most ambitious climb will collapse under the weight of distortion, because "Bad Intel" about our own worth will poison the structure before it rises.

The Architects of Nuance: Integrity as the True Carrot

Giving up to truth is liberation for the 20% who reject the comfort of convenient fictions, known as the **Architects of Nuance**. It is the way out of the Invisible Box, the escape from the slow suffocation of inherited deception. They treat *honesty as a process,* not as an occasional cleansing but as an ongoing, vigilant practice. To them, this process is a conscious weave; thread upon thread of precise observation, relentless self-correction, and deep contextual awareness. It is the discipline of seeing clearly when the Deliberate Rot would prefer they look away. They pursue *what is worthy* not as an ego trophy, but as a carrot that pulls them towards grace, integration, and towards something more than themselves.

This orientation prevents the "unfolding error," the subtle drift into misdirection that happens when the goal and the method no longer speak to each other. By bringing both into alignment, they produce Anticipatory Resonance, which is the sensation of being in harmony with reality before the result is even known. Integrity, for them, is not a moral accessory. It is a consistent Cosmic Recalibration, an ongoing realignment to self and truth.

The Guardians of Generality: Leaving the Cycle of Misalignment

For the **Guardians of Generality**, the 80%, the challenge is not seeing that alignment matters. The challenge is believing they deserve it. They often carry the weight of sunk costs in outdated beliefs, habits, and identities. To step toward truth means letting those go, and with that comes the fear of losing themselves. Rather than developing an internal sense of worth, they are drawn to outside approval, promises of miracles, and the pursuit of "big wins" that appear to be advancements but are actually positions that are prone to injury. This is *too ambitious*; a movement that is not rooted, that strains instead of builds.

Here, the loneliness of misunderstanding sets in. They work harder but feel no closer. They judge themselves by the praise of others rather than by the subtle consistency of their own convictions, deeds, and aspirations. And in so doing, they confirm the very *Bad Intel* that has left them compliant, in cycles of frustration, unable to enjoy the luxury of interior coherence. Their turning point arrives when they begin to see Integrity not as a moral obligation but as a direct path to ease, clarity, and genuine self-worth. By "showing up" consistently, by "nurturing the crawl" instead of lunging for shortcuts, they can activate the Neuro-Formulation Gateway; the shift where the body, mind, and intention move as one.

The Conscious Integrator: Becoming What You Seek

For the **Conscious Integrator / Translator**, alignment of worthiness is not optional. it is the bedrock of their function. They know that the cleanest definition of Integrity is this: *the inner and outer in perfect correspondence.* What is understood internally is expressed externally without distortion. Their work is to model that state; to live it so that others can recognize it when they see it. They lead individuals through the *Assessment as Honesty,* and they come up with the goal that is well worth the pursuit because it does not expire when the applause is over, one that reaches beyond the next transaction or the next milestone.

They carry an embodied message: *become what you are searching for.* This is not poetic abstraction. It is a lived truth that greatness is not an achievement you collect but a state of being you inhabit. The Grand Disconnect starts to fade in their presence, and Faith, the Fruit of Formed Practice, takes its place.

Then the Syntropic Future becomes more real than the present: a place where knowledge that connects rather than divides; where the light that "shines for more" is not a spotlight but a constant internal glow. The Integrator's work remains grounded, powerful, and replicable because of their humility and refusal to measure their worth by outside standards.

Integrity is not a standard you strive toward; it is the truth of yourself when nothing is pretending. Align with that, and worthiness stops being a question. It becomes the ground you walk on.

Chapter 19

The Legacy of Worthy Progress: Investment as the Seed of Integrity

"True progress is not speed, but direction rooted in devotion."

The peculiarity of our age is that even in the very concept of success, a core concept which used to be associated with hard work, talent, and an enduring sense of purpose, has been turned into a sort of performance. We are encouraged to believe that "making it" is defined by one glossy, photogenic instant: The Achievement. The scene is always framed the same way: spotlights, applause, a polished announcement. What is hidden, deliberately or carelessly, is the slow, uneven journey that makes such moments possible. This reduction is not accidental. Sometimes it is an intentional construct, a way to keep attention fixed on the symbols rather than the substance. In other situations, it is a more subdued erosion that is transmitted through culture until it is so embedded that it no longer seems like a distortion. Both versions produce the same consequence: people begin to crave shortcuts, to confuse applause with validation, and to treat patience as an outdated virtue.

When this belief takes hold, something vital is lost. The gap between consistent effort and real results, known as the Grand Disconnect, gets wider. Energy is siphoned into cycles that look productive but yield little of enduring value. In addition to being ineffective, these loops contribute to the Engineered Divide by taking human potential away from important tasks. The most perilous component of all is ingrained in them: Bad Intel, the fallacious notion that one's value is determined by outwardly apparent successes rather than by leading a life that is disciplined and in line with the truth. This flawed code quietly disarms the Action Potential of worthy progress before it can even form.

The Architects of Nuance: Precision Over Pedestal

The flaw is both dangerous and evident to the 20% who are able to see through this script, known as the Architects of Nuance. They are aware that the widely accepted definition of success is not only incomplete, but also deliberately works against the very circumstances that allow deep, lasting achievement to be possible. To them, the real definition: success is the progressive realization of a worthy goal, is not a motivational soundbite. It is a working principle. It dismantles the instant-gratification myth and replaces it with a process that welcomes what they call "the crawl and the fall." Every misstep is an opportunity for feedback and direction-refining data, not failure.

In their world, investing is a living relationship with the present rather than strict adherence to a past choice. They stay in active dialogue with their goals, using Assessment as Honesty as both a compass and course correction. By doing this, the sunk cost fallacy is broken and investment is transformed into a generative force; a Legacy Seed Sown with Integrity. Because they plant with care, their seeds take root in the deeper soil of Embodied Laws. They cultivate patiently because they know that Anticipatory Resonance-fed growth cannot be hurried. And they trust that the harvest, whenever it arrives, will be durable, resistant to the erosion of fads, market swings, and the shallow rewards that collapse when applause fades.

The Guardians of Generality: Escaping the Hollow Loop

The other 80%, the Guardians of Generality, rarely lack effort. Even though they put in a lot of overtime, they are caught in a never-

94

ending cycle. Their progress is measured by speed, by the immediacy of results, by how quickly something "pays off." When that payoff doesn't arrive on cue, the disappointment pushes them toward bigger promises, shinier offers, and faster claims. In this sense, they continue to pursue goals that are determined by the values of others, stuck in a cycle of compliant consciousness. Although the work is difficult, the objectives are illusory and designed to deliver momentary highs rather than lasting fulfillment. Working harder than ever but feeling no closer to anything that really matters is where the loneliness of misunderstanding takes root.

The turning point comes when they reframe the very definition of a worthy goal. They start to wonder if this is in line with wholism rather than pursuing scale, speed, or public recognition. They begin to ask: Does this align with Wholism? Does it nourish, or does it drain? The moment the measure shifts from "How soon will it work?" to "Does it belong to the life I am building?", investment changes shape.

It becomes not a gamble on uncertain rewards, but a "meaningful reason to try again." That shift opens the Neuro-Formulation Gateway, where intention, skill, and energy converge into coherent action. Here, Response Ability becomes more than a survival skill—it becomes the very seed of integrity, planted in ground that no longer depends on external applause to bear fruit.

The Conscious Integrator: Planting for the Future You May Never See

Investment is never just a transaction for the Conscious Integrator. It is the act of planting a seed that contains both the beginning and the unfolding of what it will become. And because they see the future as a living system rather than a fixed point, their planting is deliberate, their tending precise. They teach that a Legacy Seed Sown with Integrity is not placed in the soil for an immediate harvest. It is planted because the act itself is in harmony with truth. The core of Propagation of Praxis is the repeated, purposeful performance of the tasks that reality requires, free from the crutch of miracle thinking.

According to this perspective, investment serves as a link between form and vision. The Synaptic Dance, the interplay of skill, trust, timing, and disciplined repetition, matures into Faith as the Fruit of Formed Practice. This faith is not naïve optimism; it is the earned confidence of someone who has walked the road long enough to know what endures. Their leadership is quiet, but its effects are generational. They bring disparate efforts together to create a cohesive, long-lasting movement, mending what the Engineered Divide has ripped apart. Because they are based on principles rather than personalities, the systems they leave behind are robust enough to endure.

Thus, they reinterpret progress as a framework that will endure into the future rather than as a statement that can be made today. They know that the true measure of investment is whether it creates something that grows without you, sustained by the integrity you built into it from the beginning.

"True investment is not what you hold in your hands at the end, but what remains alive in the world when your hands are no longer there to tend it."

Chapter 20

The Genesis of Consciousness: Due Diligence in the Cradle of Partnership

"Every beginning carries its own blueprint. Attend to it with care, and you set the shape of all that follows."

The pursuit of Integrated perfection and Wholism by humans does not start with grand vision, philosophy, or policy. It begins in the smallest and most unassuming of moments, in the quiet space between a child's cry and a caregiver's response. This moment, repeated countless times in the earliest days of life, is the first test of due diligence; the active, attentive, and humble commitment to meet a genuine need with precision and care.

We often treat this as instinct, as something "automatic" in the realm of parenting. But it is far more than that. It is the first conscious weave, the earliest expression of the Embodied Protocol that will either strengthen the foundation of human potential, or compromise it from the start. If these beginnings are handled with neglect, quick fixes, or dismissiveness, then the framework for all later development rests on a broken premise.

And a foundation built on fracture will always carry the fault lines forward.

For the Architects of Nuance: the discerning 20%

For those able to see the deeper code beneath simple acts, the cry of an infant is not an inconvenience; it is a signal from the unformed world, a data point of immeasurable value. It is the first articulation of discomfort, the earliest sign of imbalance, and with it, the first opportunity for correction.

They are aware that it is a sunk cost in false comfort to ignore or cover up this cry in the name of expediency or convenience; doing so is not a neutral decision. Every skipped moment of presence, every assumption without inquiry, seeds "Bad Intel" into the child's forming reality. The patient, honest process of discovering why the cry came, and what it reveals, is their method of laying down a clean, functional layer in the consciousness of another being. This is **Assessment as Honesty** in its rawest form, a practice that transforms small moments into a foundation capable of holding the complexity of an entire life.

For the Guardians of Generality: the remaining 80%

For most, the lesson here is not about technical philosophy; it is about learning the value of showing up with constancy. The act of tending to an infant's need, patiently and without dismissal, becomes the earliest example of discipline by default, of building comfort not by avoidance of discomfort, but by walking toward it with care. This repeated engagement does more than feed or soothe; it builds trust; both in the child and in the caregiver.

It eliminates the Thirst Monster's need for immediate satisfaction and substitutes it with an increasing conviction that needs can be satisfied through process, presence, and sincere connection. By choosing inquiry over assumption, patience over reaction, and steadiness over avoidance, they unknowingly begin to replace Compliant Consciousness with the beginnings of Response Ability. And in that shift, they move closer to Wholism without yet knowing the term.

For the Conscious Integrator / Translator

For those who serve as **Conscious Integrators**, this primal relationship between parent and child is not just an emotional exchange; it is the very blueprint of consciousness itself. To "know this is consciousness from the mother while it forms consciousness of the baby" is to understand that due diligence is not only a practice, but a generative act. Every attentive moment wires the Synaptic Dance with patterns of trust, safety, and coherence.

Every unheard cry runs the risk of sowing the first seed of Deliberate Rot, guaranteeing that the child will enter later stages of life with invisible cracks in their foundation. For them, this is not sentiment; it is strategy. They know that the way we meet the earliest needs of the vulnerable sets the stage for every future partnership, every act of trust, every form of human integration to come. It is the most fundamental expression of motherhood as power, not as a role, but as origin.

"The first cries we answer are never just about the moment. They are the opening chapter of every life's architecture. And when those openings are met with diligence, humility, and truth, the light that shines for more is not a future hope. It is already here, in the room, in the arms of the one who showed up."

Chapter 21

Success as Realization: The Organic Performance of Truth and the Thirst Monster's Deception

"Success isn't about what you achieve. It's about realizing who you are in the moment."

Success in today's world is frequently determined by the titles, honors, and awards we can display to others. The shiny things are what give the impression that we've "made it." To be honest, though, this kind of success makes us feel empty. It's simple to follow these outward signs in the hopes of finding fulfilment, but when we get there, something is still lacking. We question why we don't feel complete even after obtaining everything we believed we needed. This kind of success is an illusion, and it's exactly what keeps us stuck. The next big thing, the next milestone, the next accolade, the carrot, is always just out of reach, despite the system's advice to chase it. The Thirst Monster feeds us; we are never fully content and are always looking for outside approval. We are exhausted by this cycle.

True success, however, isn't something we chase. It's something we realize. Success isn't an end goal or an external reward—it's a deep, internal recognition of who we are in the present moment. When we embrace this, we find that success isn't a destination but a way of being, an ongoing process of self-discovery and alignment.

The Architects of Nuance: Seeing Through the Illusion

For the few who see things clearly, the Architects of Nuance, it's obvious that the world's idea of success is flawed. They know success isn't about external rewards, but about inner realization. These individuals understand that when we chase success in the traditional sense, we disconnect from what truly matters: our own growth, integrity, and alignment with our deeper purpose.

The Architects are aware that true success doesn't come from the outside in. Realizing your own truth is more important than accumulating accomplishments. And without that insight, no amount of external achievement will satisfy you. Your body will rebel if you are chasing after goals that don't fit with who you really are. You won't have any drive, energy, or real progress. Burnout starts at that point. This is the "unfolding error," the endless chase after a false success that never leads to true fulfillment.

The Guardians of Generality: The Struggle with False Success

The pursuit of external success seems like an endless race to the Guardians of Generality, who make up the majority of the population. From a young age, they learn that success is determined by your accomplishments, title, and income. They exert more effort because they believe that they will feel fulfilled when they receive the next promotion or accolade.

Instead, they feel trapped. They accomplish things, but the joy is short-lived. Their desire for approval never goes away, and they end up trapped in a never-ending cycle of ambition and unfulfilled dreams. Their tendency to look outward rather than inward for approval is the epitome of the Thirst Monster.

The breakthrough happens when they realize that success is not something they have to chase; it's already within them. Success isn't about what others think—it's about showing up, being authentic, and embracing the journey of becoming. When they stop seeking external validation and start realizing their own value, the emptiness starts to fade. True success is found not in accolades but in living your truth, in taking each step with integrity, and in trusting the process.

The Conscious Integrator / Translator: Leading the Shift Toward True Success

For the Conscious Integrator, the task is to help people see that the way we define success is backward. Success is not about what we achieve or how we're recognized; it is about realizing who we are and aligning with that truth. The work of the Integrator is to help others shift from the illusion of external success to the realization of internal truth.

The Integrator helps people step away from the idea that success is something to be obtained. Instead, it is something we realize in every moment, through living authentically. They show others that true success is not a trophy or a title, it is the daily practice of living in alignment with your values, showing up with integrity, and trusting the process. The Integrator helps reframe the false pursuit of success and brings people back to their true source of fulfillment.

When people start to understand that success is an internal realization, not an external achievement, their whole approach to life shifts. The "bad intel" they have been fed, the idea that success is something to chase, begins to dissolve, and they start to experience true fulfillment in the journey, not just in the destination. The Conscious Integrator's work is to guide people toward the realization that success is not something we get, it is something we become.

Conclusion: Success as Realization

Real success is about the realization of your potential, not the pursuit of external validation. It's not about chasing after accolades, titles, or achievements. True success is found in the moment when we align with our own truth and realize that we are already enough.

The Thirst Monster will always try to convince us that success is something we need to pursue outside of ourselves, but the reality is that success is already within us. It is not a distant dream; it is right here, in the present moment, ready to be realized. True fulfillment comes not from reaching a goal but from understanding that the journey itself, when lived authentically, is the real reward. Success is not something you achieve; it is something you realize. And once you realize it, you unlock a new way of being in the world, where the pursuit of external validation is no longer necessary, and your life becomes an ongoing performance of truth, growth, and alignment.

Chapter 22

Acceptance as an Axis: The Width of Wit in the Reel of Reality

"The reel is not broken by contradiction; it widens in it, and in that widening, the whole of reality is revealed."

Acceptance has long been mistaken for surrender. But the acceptance spoken here is no retreat. It is an axis; an orientation that steadies us when the fractures of perception pull in opposite directions. This is not the silence of defeat; it is the still point around which true integration turns.

Acceptance as an Axis is the capacity to hold the paradox that you were right, and so was your friend; that both light and shadow belong to the same horizon; that contradiction does not destroy truth, but discloses its deeper layers. This is the antidote to the Grand Disconnect. It does not erase difference, but repositions it as the fertile ground where Action Potential germinates. Here, humility is the hinge. Without it, we collapse into rigidity; with it, the reel of reality comes alive again.

The Architects of Nuance: Holding the Contradiction

For the 20% who refuse to be fooled, Acceptance as an Axis is not softness but discipline. They know that reality is not a fixed singularity but a reel; spinning, shifting, threaded with contradictions that are not errors but openings. Their unfooled eye discerns that "The Truth" is itself a closure, a lock, a narrowing of the reel into the rigid frame that feeds the Deliberate Rot.

Instead, they embrace the Language of Paradox and Contradiction, seeing in it not confusion but coherence waiting to be revealed. They weave opposing strands into a Synaptic Dance, where seeming rivals become partners in resonance. This is the conscious weave that restores Anticipatory Resonance, transforming conflict into synthesis, and fear into imagination. For them, acceptance is not the loss of position but the gaining of width; not a collapse into vagueness but the expansion into wholeness.

The Guardians of Generality: Struggling with the Width

For the 80%, the Guardians of Generality, acceptance feels impossible. Their Compliant Consciousness has been conditioned to crave binaries, to seek singular beginnings, singular endings, singular victories. They are taught that if one is right, the other must be wrong; that truth is fragile, unable to hold tension. This refusal of duality is not malice; it is habit. Yet it traps them in endless cycles of conflict. They fight over fragments because they cannot yet see the reel. Here, *Bad Intel* is not only deception but structure: a code that programs them to believe contradiction is chaos, when in fact, contradiction is the doorway to Wholism.

The shift comes in the Sacred Pause. When Guardians learn to slow the reflex of reaction, to nurse the crawl instead of lunging for false certainty, the anxiety eases. They glimpse that both sides of a story may be true within their own frame. This recognition does not weaken them; it steadies them. In that moment, Response Ability awakens, and the loneliness of misunderstanding begins to dissolve. Acceptance becomes the bridge across the Engineered Divide.

The Conscious Integrator / Translator: The Living Pivot

For the Integrator, Acceptance as an Axis is not a concept; it is their posture, their Nobel function. They embody the humility to say: *I did not know, and should not have known yet.* They reveal that wisdom is not the possession of one side, but the living reel where both belong. Their task is to guide others into this recognition, not by force, but by modeling. They transform fragmented justice into functional wisdom, teaching that paradox is not to be feared but to be embraced as the place where integration takes root. They show that acceptance is not the erasure of conviction, but its enlargement: the moment where contradiction becomes coherence.

The Integrator lives the reel, weaving Architect and Guardian into a shared axis. They restore the reel of reality to its flowing form, dismantling the Invisible Box by proving, in their own being, that opposites can coexist without canceling one another. In this lived demonstration, Wholism ceases to be feared; it becomes possible. Faith as the Fruit of Formed Practice becomes tangible, and the Genesis of Action is reborn in Integrity.

Conclusion: The Reel Restored

Acceptance as an Axis is the pivot where fragmentation loosens. For the Architects, it is the mastery of paradox; for the Guardians, it is the first step beyond binaries; for the Integrators, it is the bridge itself. Together, it restores the reel of reality, fluid, dynamic, wide enough to hold the contradictions of life without tearing apart.

In this acceptance, the Action Potential is freed from the cages of false certainty. The Grand Disconnect begins to mend. And the horizon, once divided, becomes whole again.

"To accept is not to yield. It is to widen. And in the widening, the reel of reality spins true."

But what spins must also root. What widens must also sow. The reel, if true, must turn to soil.

106

Chapter 23

The Unplannable Harvest: Nurturing Complexity Through Formed Being

"The seed cannot be scheduled; it is formed in silence, and its harvest is the echo of that unseen formation."

If acceptance widens the reel, then formation deepens the soil. Complexity is not a puzzle to be solved, nor a battlefield to be conquered; it is a field to be cultivated, an unfolding that cannot be forced into submission. Yet the world insists otherwise: chart it, control it, engineer it into predictability. This is the Invisible Box at work; the false promise of *The* solution, the *Bad Intel* that codes the mind into rigidity, persuading us that mastery lies in perfect planning.

But reality laughs at such hubris. Complexity does not move in straight lines; it grows, spirals, braids, weaves, and resists domestication. To meet it requires not blueprints but *formation*. To engage it demands that we do not merely "plan ahead" but rather sow form into our very being, shaping the vessel so that whatever fruit emerges, we are ready to hold it. This is the radical redefinition: planning as ontology, preparation not of itinerary but of interior soil.

The Architects of Nuance: Sowing Form into Being

For the 20% who discern, the Architects of Nuance, this recognition becomes the central act of discipline. Planning is not projection into the future; it is the patient weaving of form in the present. They sow themselves into alignment with the reel of reality. Their plans are not fragile documents that collapse in contact with surprise. Their blueprints are *embodied protocols*; habits that endure turbulence, patterns that remain supple in chaos. Their cultivation is silent, often invisible to the world, but it is relentless. They train not only their intellect but their disposition. They rehearse humility. They practice patience. They refine their posture until it aligns with Syntropic Resonance: the principle that order, when formed correctly, emerges organically from within.

Thus, when others see only chaos, the Architects perceive pattern. They do not fear the storm, for they have become the vessel that can ride it. They do not attempt to control complexity; they become complexity, resonating with its hidden rhythms. The Unplannable Harvest is not threat but ally. It is the confirmation that what was sown in silence now flowers in form. Their mastery is not external prediction but internal formation. They embody the paradox: that the surest plan for the future is to become the kind of being who can hold whatever the future brings.

The Guardians of Generality: Trapped by the Quick Yield

For the 80%, the Guardians of Generality, complexity feels like betrayal. They have been programmed to equate planning with control, outcomes with worth, and speed with success. Their Compliant Consciousness longs for quick yield, immediate validation, the illusion of mastery without the patience of cultivation. But this is fragile. Quick growth burns out roots. Over-ambition fractures the vessel. In chasing the carrot of instant result, they injure their own becoming. Their fear of delay becomes its own rot. This is the loneliness of misunderstanding: believing themselves abandoned by progress when in fact they are only resisting the crawl.

Yet their prison is not final. A shift becomes possible in the Sacred Pause. When Guardians slow their reflex to demand harvest before its season, they discover the power of soil. When they begin to prepare foundations, choosing environments that nourish, tending to Integrity, investing in slow formation, their striving softens. Anxiety, once gnawing, loosens its grip.

This is their Neuro-Formulation Gateway: realizing that the measure of success is not speed of outcome but faithfulness of cultivation. When they trust form over yield, striving transforms into grounded progression. Faith as the Fruit of Formed Practice arises naturally, no longer fragile, no longer frantic. In this soil of persistence, the Guardians discover what the Architects already knew: harvest is not something you seize. It is something you *become ready to receive*.

The Conscious Integrator / Translator: Living Blueprints

For the Integrator, this chapter reveals their deepest paradox. They carry the burden of the Impossibility of Dual Presence: to be fully *here*, aware of current limits, present struggles, unfinished soil, and simultaneously *there*, alive in the vision of Wholism, already embodying future fruit. This tension could fracture the untrained. But for the Integrator, it is their Nobel function. They learn to inhabit both without collapsing either. They stand as living blueprints, embodying praxis not as rigid projection but as fluid propagation of form.

Their role is not only to cultivate themselves but to reveal to others that complexity is not an enemy but an echo. The very tangle of contradiction, delay, or difficulty is the intricate way the seeds were formed. They decode the "noise" and reveal it as structure in hiding. They translate despair into pattern, confusion into coherence. In their posture, others glimpse possibility. The Integrator demonstrates that greatness is never engineered by control; it is cultivated through surrender to form. By aligning themselves with organic processes, they dismantle *Bad Intel* about rigid planning. They show that emergence is not an accident but a fruit of fidelity.

Their humility releases collective Action Potential. Their wholeness allows fragmented efforts to braid together. They are not simply leaders; they are fertile fields, carrying the harvest before it has even ripened.

The Larger Lesson: Soil Over Schedule

The wisdom of the Unplannable Harvest is this: what you form is what you reap. The soil of your being determines the fruit of your becoming.

- For the Architects, this is mastery; sowing form as discipline until it becomes second nature.
- For the Guardians, this is liberation; releasing ambition into patience and finding peace in the process.
- For the Integrators, this is mission; embodying the very coherence that complexity seemed to resist.

Harvest cannot be forced into calendars. It is not secured by maps or strategies. It comes in its own time, born of invisible processes, nurtured by diligence and humility.

Acceptance widened the reel. Now cultivation deepens the soil. And in that soil, patience does its quiet work until fruit ripens in its season.

Conclusion: The Harvest Beyond Maps

Complexity is not solved. It is cultivated. It is sown in silence, watered in discipline, and reaped in form. The Unplannable Harvest is not about control but coherence, not about outcomes but ontology.

To plan for it is futile; to *form* for it is essential. The true harvest is not what you gain; it is what you become in the process of waiting, shaping, tending.

"Do not plan for the harvest; sow your being, and the harvest will plan itself."

Chapter 24

Faith as the Fruit of Formed Practice: The Dance of Remembered Promise

"Faith is not blind belief; it is the rhythm of form remembering itself."

Having sown the soil of formation, we arrive at the harvest beyond maps. And the fruit revealed is not simply outcome, not simply achievement, but Faith, not as doctrine, not as demand, but as the felt resonance of practiced form. This is the Dance of Remembered Promise, where the effort of weaving, the patience of tending, and the humility of formation converge into something more enduring than yield.

Faith here is not an imposed creed. It is an *emergent confidence*, authored not by slogans but by the living evidence of discipline. It is the undeniable rhythm of Reality answering back to form. Faith, in this sense, is the proof of Action Potential realized. It is the universe whispering: *"What you practiced has become who you are."*

The Architects of Nuance: Faith as Ontological Actualization

For the Architects of Nuance, the discerning 20%, Faith is not fragile belief; it is the ontological actualization of consistent form. They do not gamble on outcomes. They embody processes until the processes themselves speak back in rhythm. Every practice, every discipline, every embodied protocol becomes a feedback loop with Reality. And the loop itself is Faith. Their conviction is not hope without evidence; it is evidence made living. The soil they cultivated, the habits they formed, the humility they sustained, all of it flowers into a lived certainty: the world coheres, not by accident, but because they have aligned themselves with its laws.

This is why their Faith is unshaken by storms. It is not a brittle fantasy but a formed resonance. They trust emergence not because they wish to, but because their experience has confirmed its truth. They perceive the miracle of organic growth, fruit that no hand engineered, yet which their diligence has undeniably invited.

Thus, their Faith is no longer belief. It is Syntropic Resonance embodied, a living assurance that the Legacy Seed, sown in Integrity, will always bloom in its season.

The Guardians of Generality: Faith as Antidote to the Thirst

For the Guardians of Generality, the 80%, this re-formed Faith becomes the antidote to the Thirst Monster, the unending hunger for external carrots, the restlessness of blind striving. They have been taught that Faith means outsourcing belief to a system, an authority, a trick. But this is *Bad Intel*.

True Faith arises not from surrendering judgment but from cultivating discipline. It is not belief imposed from without, but conviction generated from within. For them, Faith begins simply, humbly: the act of showing up, of counting their persistence as victory, of giving themselves credit for forming when results still hide. This quiet mantra, "I showed up, and therefore I am becoming," rewires their Compliant Consciousness into resilience.

And slowly, the fruit ripens. Faith ceases to be a desperate plea to unseen forces and becomes instead a natural byproduct of practice. Discipline by default builds comfort. Comfort builds courage. Courage builds consistency. And consistency births Faith; not fragile, not borrowed, but rooted. Here lies their **Neuro-Formulation Gateway**: Faith as lived assurance, not imposed illusion. This anchors them against the loneliness of misunderstanding. It frees them from the injustice of poor language that promised quick fixes. And it grounds them in a Response Ability that does not break under pressure.

For the Guardians, Faith is no longer thirst. It is water. It quenches because it flows from within.

The Conscious Integrator / Translator: Faith as Blueprint of Wholism

For the Conscious Integrator / Translator, this is the culmination. Their task is not only to cultivate Faith in themselves but to model Faith as a system; Faith in the weave itself, Faith in integration, Faith in Wholism as the only soil of a worthy future. Here, Faith becomes the remembered promise of the system: that consistent weaving yields coherence, that humility yields fruit, that patience yields strength. The Integrator must embody this assurance, not to preach it, but to *become it*. In their posture, others glimpse the truth: Faith is not magic; it is memory. It is Reality remembering itself through us.

Their Nobel function is to demonstrate that the Dance of Remembered Promise is not an illusion but evidence. It is what happens when fragments cohere, when Action Potential is unified, when integrity replaces trickery. Their Faith is catalytic; it dismantles *Bad Intel* about external validation and replaces it with the rhythm of lived emergence. In them, Faith ceases to be private comfort. It becomes public architecture. They are living blueprints, modeling a Syntropic Future where fragmentation heals, complexity flourishes democratically, and the Grand Disconnect is overcome.

The Larger Lesson: Faith as Emergent Fruit

Faith is not something you choose. It is something you *become.*

- For the Architects: it is mastery; certainty born of embodied protocol.
- For the Guardians: it is healing; relief from thirst, assurance born of showing up.
- For the Integrators: it is blueprint; Faith as a system that coheres the collective.

Faith cannot be fabricated by willpower. It must ripen in the soil of practice. It is the fruit of formed being, the Dance of Remembered Promise, the harvest that proves the soil was true.

Conclusion: Faith as Remembered Rhythm

Faith, finally, is the rhythm that cannot be faked. It is the undeniable cadence of form ripened into fruit. It is not blind. It is not imposed. It is not fragile.

It is memory. It is harvest. It is wholeness remembering itself.

And so, as we step beyond the soil of Chapter 23, we realize: the ultimate confirmation of formation is Faith. The fruit of practice is not simply success; it is the assurance that we are already aligned with Reality.

Faith is not belief. Faith is formed memory, alive in us.

"Faith is not what you cling to; it is what clings to you after you have formed yourself into truth."

Chapter 25

Propagation of Praxis: The Art of Transference and the Collective Ascent

"Truth that is not shared collapses into itself.
But the truth that is carried with care becomes seed for the many."

The work of integration, if it ends with the individual, remains unfinished. To see is not enough. To practice faithfully, though necessary, is still not enough. At some point, the question arrives; quietly, insistently: *Can what has been formed in me take root in another without distortion?*

That question is the essence of **Propagation of Praxis.** It is the final test of Integrity. It asks not only whether insight can be kept, but whether it can be handed across the gap; from Architect to Guardian, from one life to another, without losing its shape. This is not dissemination. Dissemination is easy: scatter ideas, publish them, "share" them in the shallow sense. Propagation is harder. It requires not just words but embodiment, not just transfer but transference. The form itself must move with the content. Praxis, if it is true, must be transferable.

This is why the Propagation of Praxis is not a luxury add-on to the journey; it is the journey's confirmation. If integration remains private, it withers into ornament. But when it travels, when it is carried with humility and rooted in others, it becomes the antidote to the Grand Disconnect. It transforms knowledge from something admired at a distance into something lived together.

The Architects of Nuance: Bearing the Weight of Translation

For the **Architects of Nuance,** the 20% who have cultivated the unfooled eye, the challenge is not whether they can see. They already see: the fracture, the Invisible Box, the quiet tyranny of the definite article *"The."* Their challenge is whether they can bear the weight of translation. They know how fragile their insights are, how much patience it took to reach them. To simply "hand over" the finished vision risks creating new distortion, a Guardian overwhelmed, or worse, attempting shortcuts that collapse into the same traps. The temptation is strong: to impress with brilliance, to deliver the conclusion rather than the crawl. But to do so is to betray the process that birthed the truth.

Thus, the Architect must discipline themselves a second time. The first discipline was the excavation of truth; the second is its careful delivery. They must learn to simplify without dilution, to present clarity without collapsing complexity into cliché. And above all, they must resist the impulse to make disciples of themselves rather than practitioners of reality. When they succeed, they plant seeds rather than monuments. Their gift ceases to be private sophistication and becomes shared soil. This is their legacy: a seed of Integrity sown not for applause, but for the endurance of Wholism.

The Guardians of Generality: Reclaiming Agency Through Praxis

For the **Guardians of Generality,** the 80%, Propagation of Praxis is often the first taste of genuine agency. Most of their lives have been conducted within conditioning, "mailed by it," trapped in cycles of compliant consciousness. They have been trained to treat authority as truth and quick fixes as progress. Their hunger for coherence has been exploited by Bad Intel, leaving them restless, lonely, and half-blind to their own potential.

But when praxis is transferred with care, not as abstract principle but as *doable practice*, something shifts. A Guardian learns that nourishing food changes their energy more than any other "miracle diet." That unbroken rest restores them more than a stimulant. That tending a craft patiently over time produces confidence more enduring than applause.

These may sound small. But in a culture addicted to shortcuts, the small is revolutionary. Each simple act is a breach in the Engineered Divide. Each time a Guardian sees a functional result, fatigue lifted, confidence rebuilt, clarity replacing confusion, the spell of deception weakens. Their cravings, once hijacked by the Thirst Monster, are redirected into the pursuit of *what endures*. Here humility is not weakness. It is the courage to engage with the crawl, to take instruction without shame, to admit: "I did not know, but now I can learn." In that admission, agency is reclaimed. And with agency, the possibility of wholeness begins.

The Conscious Integrator: The Living Bridge

For the **Conscious Integrator / Translator**, Propagation of Praxis is not an optional function. It is their center. They are the bridge between Architect and Guardian, not merely a communicator, but a *living conduit*. Their chief tool is the Lexicon of Integration. This is more than vocabulary; it is the deliberate crafting of language that does not divide. The Integrator refuses to patronize with oversimplification, and equally refuses to obscure with elitism. They speak in a tongue that honors both complexity and accessibility.

This is why their presence matters more than their words. In the Integrator's posture, Guardians see that clarity can exist without condescension, and Architects see that translation need not mean betrayal. The Integrator embodies Acceptance as an Axis, holding contradiction without collapse, standing steady in paradox until both sides recognize themselves in the whole. Through them, praxis does not merely transfer; it propagates. It spreads not as doctrine but as atmosphere, not as a rigid system but as a living rhythm. In their way of being, the lonely discover community, the fractured glimpse Wholism, and the Engineered Divide begins to dissolve.

Conclusion: Praxis as Collective Ascent

Propagation of Praxis is not about replication; it is about continuity. The goal is not to produce carbon copies but to cultivate coherence, a rhythm that can move through a community, a generation, a future. When the Architect translates with humility, when the Guardian receives with courage, and when the Integrator embodies the bridge, a new architecture emerges. It is not the triumph of one brilliant mind, but the rising-together of many.

This is what dismantles the Deliberate Rot: not rebellion alone, not insight alone, but the slow, shared embodiment of truth across differences. Propagation is the proof that truth belongs not to the few but to the many, not to the elite but to the whole.

For the Architect, it is the test of translation.

For the Guardian, it is the reclamation of agency.

For the Integrator, it is the living bridge.

And for all, it is the horizon of ascent, the moment when praxis ceases to be private and becomes the pulse of a people.

"Truth that is carried hand to hand outlives the one who first held it. It becomes legacy, not because it was believed, but because it was lived."

Chapter 26

The Unfooled Eye: Radical Acceptance as the Glimpse of the True Miracle

"Miracles are not interruptions of reality, but the moment we finally see what was always there, hidden beneath the disguise."

Naming the Breach

The task before us is not to wage war on deception with the same blunt force it used against us. The work is subtler, deeper, and ultimately more courageous. Our purpose is to **name the breach**, to acknowledge with precision the wound that has been cultivated through centuries of distortion, misdirection, and sleight of hand. The so-called "Severed Genesis" and all other engineered myths are not merely misinformation but are carefully calculated performances in which to cover the organic truth of the relationship and genesis.

To name the breach is to call the illusion what it is: a performance that concealed wholeness, a curtain drawn to suggest separation where only connection ever existed. This naming is not destruction, it is reclamation. It is the refusal to be a silent participant in fabricated reality. When we turn toward the uncomfortable truth with humility, we break the curse of unconscious compliance. At that point, the functional consciousness is reestablished, and the true extent of Action Potential starts to take place.

For the Architects of Nuance: Radical Acceptance as Craft

For the few who carry the unfooled eye, the 20% who will not be deceived by surface appearances, this chapter marks a discipline of radical acceptance. It is not resignation, nor is it bitterness. It is the clear-eyed acknowledgment that deception occurred, that humanity has been subject to layers of intentional distortion, and that this is part of the reality we must face.

This acceptance does not weaken; it strengthens. It gives the Architect permission to see without flinching, to embrace the precision of truth, no matter how unwelcomed it first feels. They know that the miracle is not found in denial but in patience; patience with the process, patience with reality's rhythm, patience with themselves. Every detail, every fracture, every distortion contains clues about the larger design.

Armed with Anticipatory Resonance, they discern the subtle signals that reveal hidden patterns. Through due diligence, they learn not only how the deception was planted but how even false seeds were formed within reality's soil. Their unfooled eye discerns the full spectrum, exposing the Deliberate Rot and the Engineered Divide without becoming trapped by them. By this clarity, they help clear the ground for Syntropic Resonance; the natural unfolding of coherence when lies lose their hold. Radical acceptance becomes their miracle: the recognition that truth was never destroyed, only obscured, waiting for eyes that could finally see it.

For the Guardians of Generality: The Gentle Unveiling

For the Guardians, the 80% who live under the fog of conditioned perception, the task is harder, though no less essential. To them, the very idea of dismantling deception often feels frightening, destabilizing, or even dangerous. Their Compliant Consciousness prefers surface appearances, where things look settled, safe, and familiar. It is in this preference that they remain vulnerable to the sleight of hand, the cultural magic trick that convinces them falsehood is reality and reality is unreachable.

The real breakthrough comes not in grand rebellion, but in something far gentler: slowing down. Through what we have called *Assessment as Honesty*, the Guardian learns to pause and look closely, to study the supposed "barrier" until its cracks become visible. What once seemed an impenetrable wall is revealed as a clever construction, a deterrent rather than a true block.

This revelation is liberating. It does not overwhelm; it comforts. They begin to see that the "uncrossable" was never truly there, that their imagination was mailed shut by conditioning. Each act of careful seeing restores their Response Ability, moving them out of the loneliness of misunderstanding into the confidence of participation. Their humility in questioning appearances becomes the seed of courage, freeing them from the cycles of Bad Intel that once coded them into silence.

For the Conscious Integrator: Liberation Architecture

And then there are the Integrators, the translators, the bridge-builders, those whose Nobel function is to design liberation architecture. For them, this chapter is less an insight than a commission. They understand something vital: the original truth of creation, the organic power of motherhood, the wholeness of relationship; these were never truly destroyed. They were only hidden, veiled, re-coded into obscurity by intentional erasure.

The Integrator's work is to help others reclaim sight. They guide the act of naming the breach, not with condemnation but with compassion, not with dogma but with patience. Their gift is to restore confidence that wholeness was always here, beneath the distortions, waiting to be remembered.

Through them, radical acceptance spreads. It becomes less about exposing lies and more about revealing the unbroken truth that still pulses at the center of reality. In their guidance, humanity learns that deception loses its power the moment it is seen for what it is. That moment, when the fog dissolves and clarity returns, is the glimpse of the true miracle.

The Integrator reminds us that a miracle is not a spectacle. It is the quiet return of wholeness after centuries of fracture, the dawning awareness that truth never left. It was simply waiting to be seen.

Conclusion: The Glimpse of the True Miracle

The unfooled eye is not merely sight; it is courage, humility, and radical acceptance woven into one. To name the breach is to reclaim consciousness, to stop being complicit in illusions, and to step back into the organic flow of Wholism.

For the Architect, it is a discipline of clarity.

For the Guardian, it is a gentle unveiling.

For the Integrator, it is liberation architecture.

Together, they prepare humanity for the Syntropic Future, where deception no longer codes our perception, and Action Potential is no longer trapped in unconscious loops.

The miracle is not some distant interruption, descending from elsewhere. It is the recognition that reality itself, once unveiled, is more miraculous than any fabrication.

"The true miracle is not what arrives from beyond, but what was always here, revealed in the moment we refuse to be fooled any longer."

Chapter 27

The Sacred Pause: Nurturing the Crawl and Halting the Race

"The miracle is not in how fast we arrive, but in learning to dwell with each step until it teaches us who we are becoming."

The Race and Its Deceptions

Modern life insists on speed. It is the hum of the race: a frantic push forward, rarely questioned, driven by the **Thirst Monster's hunger** and by illusions dressed up as instant miracles. The pressure to keep moving, to reach the next milestone, to embody the polished image of "The Success" leaves little space for organic growth. Instead of foundations being tended with care, they are skipped or patched over, producing fragile lives, shallow systems, and fractured communities.

This obsession with racing is no accident. It is cultivated. It reinforces the Engineered Divide, ensuring that humanity never reaches its deeper Action Potential. The deception at work, the Bad Intel we are fed, is that constant speed equals progress. But what it really codes into us is exhaustion, shallow foundations, and the inability to sustain humility. Instead of strength, it produces collapse. Instead of freedom, it perpetuates dependency.

For the Architects of Nuance: Nursing the Crawl

For the 20% who see beneath the surface, the **Architects of Nuance**, the Sacred Pause is not weakness but wisdom. Their unfooled eye recognizes the profound necessity of "**nursing the crawl before you walk.**" This is more than patience; it is a form of **Anticipatory Resonance** applied to growth itself.

Every stutter, wobble, and slow repetition turns into data rather than a failure. Each moment of awkward practice is a thread in the conscious weave of becoming. The Architect knows that skipping steps does not accelerate progress; it sabotages it. What endures is built in increments, deliberate, simple, and foundational. They align their process with Embodied Laws, knowing that miracles are not sudden explosions but the steady emergence of truth over time.

In refusing the lure of shortcuts, they honor the integrity of growth. Although the race may shine with promises, the Architect understands that true power is developed through patience, hard work, and stillness. It is from this posture that the Unplannable Harvest can ripen in its season.

For the Guardians of Generality: Stopping the Race

For the **Guardians of Generality,** the 80% caught in the tide of cultural conditioning, the race feels inevitable. They are told from childhood that worth is found in speed, in acceleration, in always moving "ahead." But the truth is harsher: this ceaseless race leaves them restless, drained, and unfulfilled. Ambition becomes over-ambition. Effort leads to injury: physical, emotional, or spiritual. What remains is exhaustion and the loneliness of misunderstanding.

Here lies their deception: the Thirst Monster promises relief through shortcuts, but delivers only deeper emptiness. And so, they run harder, chasing what was never there.

The breakthrough is deceptively simple: stop the race. Step out of the illusion that progress must be hurried. Discover the stability and comfort that comes from deliberate process, from slowing down enough to feel the rhythm of true growth. This conscious deceleration becomes a doorway into the Neuro-Formulation Gateway, where the mind, body, and spirit find coherence. In this pause, humility returns. And with humility, **Faith as the Fruit of Formed Practice** can take root, faith not in tricks, but in the steady truth of one's own process.

Without valuing this process, the Guardian remains coded by Bad Intel, locked in cycles of burnout. With it, however, they learn that miracles were always about alignment, patience, and simplicity rather than speed.

For the Conscious Integrator: Modeling the Pause

For the **Conscious Integrator / Translator**, the Sacred Pause is not a suggestion. It is their Nobel function. They clearly recognize that the desire for quick fixes and shortcuts is not just a personal weakness, rather a cultural symptom of Compliant Consciousness, a system that values results over integrity and speed over substance.

Their essential task is to model the opposite: to show that slowing down is not regression but revolution. By creating spaces of pause, whether the "90 seconds of thought" that interrupts habit, or the longer rhythms of diligence, they give others the chance to recalibrate. They teach that planning is not about control, but about forming integrity.

In this way, the Integrator helps heal the Grand Disconnect. Their presence dismantles the illusion of racing and invites others into the rhythm of deliberate growth, into the Synaptic Dance of true integration. In their humility, they reveal that pausing is not weakness; it is power, the power to restore Wholism, to cultivate sustainable potency, and to prepare for the Syntropic Future where knowledge unites rather than divides.

Conclusion: The Power of Stillness

The Sacred Pause is more than a tactic. It is an axis around which genuine growth turns.

For the Architect, it is nursing the crawl, honoring the integrity of progression.

For the Guardian, it is stopping the race, finding rest where exhaustion once ruled.

For the Integrator, it is modeling pause itself, guiding others into coherence.

Waiting is the most radical action in a world where shortcuts are alluring. To value diligence over speed, humility over illusion, and process over spectacle. According to the Sacred Pause, miracles are not hurried; rather, they develop gradually as a result of endurance, presence, and the guts to stop running.

"In the stillness where the race is halted, the miracle of true becoming finally has space to arrive."

At the close of Chapter 27, we spoke of the Sacred Pause, the radical act of halting the race, of nursing the crawl before rushing into leaps that fracture us. That chapter reminded us that genuine progress is never born from speed or shortcuts, but from patience, humility, and the willingness to walk in rhythm with reality. Yet, this pause is not merely a personal practice. It also draws our attention to something deeper: the way entire civilizations have forgotten the crawl, erased the foundations, and re-scripted beginnings.

The race we run today is not just cultural haste; it is the symptom of a much older distortion, the loss of our original blueprint. The Sacred Pause steadies us long enough to notice the absence. And once we notice it, a harder truth emerges: humanity has not only ignored its roots but has allowed them to be systematically erased. Stories of abrupt, isolated origins have supplanted what was once organic, embodied, and rooted in process. These lies, which have been perpetuated for centuries, have left us disconnected from our own physiology, creativity, and shared origins.

126

This realization brings us to the next step in our journey: the recovery of what was lost. To pause is to recognize where we are. To reclaim the Erased Blueprint is to remember where we come from.

Chapter 28

The Erased Blueprint: When Reality Forgets Its Roots

"To forget our beginnings is to lose the pattern of becoming; the blueprint erased is the harvest undone."

The Foundations We Neglect

The most fundamental truths of life are not abstract theories or complex philosophies. They are rooted in the body, in the primal realities of breath, nourishment, rest, and rhythm. From these physiological essentials flows every higher dimension of human growth, integrity, discipline, structure, articulation, and principled being. This is not metaphor. It is the tangible, living architecture of Embodied Laws: the recognition that authentic consciousness begins not in lofty ideas, but in the patient tending of basic needs.

This is the true meaning of "crawl before you walk." It is the process that lays down the Organic Foundation, upon which every genuine unfolding depends. To bypass this foundation is to code error into the very fabric of our perception, creating distortions that compromise Action Potential before it can even take form. And at its core, this foundation is authored by humility, the willingness to honor the slow truth of process. Without humility, the blueprint bends. Without humility, the roots are forgotten.

The Erasure of Organic Reference

Yet somewhere in humanity's story, a breach occurred. What should have been honored was erased. This erasure was not an accident; it was an intentional deception, a deliberate redrafting of origins that severed our connection to natural processes.

This is what I call the **"Erasure of Organic Reference."** Ancient narratives began to present miracles not as the slow flowering of process, but as instantaneous acts; sudden, detached, male-centered events. Stories such as the "rib from Adam" or the "immaculate conception that negates the role of wives" became cultural cornerstones. These tales displaced the organic, generative, feminine power of co-creation, replacing it with isolated acts of divine command.

The cost of this distortion is profound. The Severed Genesis is more than myth; it is a broken premise encoded into culture. By displacing natural co-creation, it turned the flow of life into a hierarchy, an engineered structure of control. In this system, humility is silenced, origins are rewritten, and the natural weave of process is replaced by a brittle singularity, "The" beginning, "The" authority. This is Bad Intel at its root: a deception so deep it warps our very sense of reality, reinforcing the Engineered Divide and feeding the Deliberate Rot across generations.

For the Architects of Nuance: Seeing the Broken Premise

For the **Architects of Nuance,** the 20% whose eyes are trained to see beneath illusions, the Erasure of Organic Reference stands out as one of the great betrayals of thought. They perceive how the portrayal of miracles as sudden and external undermines the reality of creation as diligence, patience, and process. Their unfooled eye discerns the deep trick at work: when origins are recast as instantaneous and male-centric, imagination itself is diminished. The human capacity for Anticipatory Resonance, the ability to perceive the patterns of becoming, is crippled. What should inspire alignment with natural design instead fosters disorientation and misdirection.

The Architect recognizes this as a systemic unfolding error. By severing organic beginnings, humanity has inherited a distorted framework where truth seems fragmented and unreachable. The "uncrossable obstacle" is not physical but narrative: a blueprint erased, leaving collective greatness trapped behind illusions.

For the Guardians of Generality: Living in the Disconnect

For the **Guardians of Generality**, the 80% shaped by this erasure, the consequences are painfully lived. Cut off from organic reference, they inherit a profound Grand Disconnect. Without the blueprint, their perception of reality becomes detached from its roots. They are left in what might be called an Unconceptualized Gap, unable to access the food of Anticipatory Resonance, unable to orient themselves to the natural rhythm of growth. Their well-meaning efforts are sincere, but they are built upon fractured premises. The result is exhaustion, confusion, and the endless pursuit of fragmented solutions.

They strive harder and harder, yet remain misaligned. Their ambition grows "too ambitious," leaving them injury-prone, burned out, frustrated, and trapped in cycles of striving without direction. Their **Compliant Consciousness** accepts the fabricated narratives as truth because the organic reference that might expose the deception has been systematically erased.

This is the cruelest part of the trick: they are not lazy or unwilling, but misled at the root. With Bad Intel as input, their Action Potential is coded into distortion. The loneliness of misunderstanding deepens, and humility, the very key to reorienting, remains out of reach.

For the Conscious Integrator: Reclaiming the Blueprint

For the **Conscious Integrator / Translator**, the task is monumental yet essential: to help humanity reclaim its erased blueprint. Their work is to expose the trick for what it is; not to shame, but to reveal, patiently and clearly, that genuine miracles are process, not magic tricks. They point to the Embodied Laws, to the rhythms of agriculture, to the patience of biological evolution, to the organic wisdom of motherhood, as living examples of what has always been true. By decoding the Severed Genesis, they restore the integrity of origins and empower others to see that creative power was never lost, only obscured.

In this role, the Integrator becomes a bridge, guiding Guardians to rediscover what the Architects already perceive. They reveal that the womb of creation; the power to nurture, generate, and co-weave reality, is not symbolic but literal. It is the ground upon which Wholism can rise, the soil where Faith as the Fruit of Formed Practice takes root.

Their humility in naming these truths becomes the catalyst for healing. Through this reclamation, individuals and communities can reorient themselves to the Organic Foundation. In doing so, humanity regains the possibility of Syntropic Resonance, of collective integration, of a future no longer fractured by false beginnings.

Conclusion: Remembering the Roots

The erased blueprint was never truly gone; it was only obscured.

For the Architect, the task is to expose the broken premise.

For the Guardian, it is to rediscover the forgotten roots beneath the confusion.

For the Integrator, it is to reclaim and propagate the blueprint as shared soil.

To forget our origins is to live disoriented, fractured, chasing illusions. But to remember them, to honor the organic reference, is to rebuild the integrity of life itself. Only in that remembrance does true Action Potential emerge, and only then does the possibility of Wholism and Integrated Perfection become real.

"When we return to the roots, the erased blueprint redraws itself, not as history recovered, but as life remembered in its wholeness."

The work of reclaiming the erased blueprint cannot remain only as memory or recognition. To see where we have been misled is the first step; to walk a new way is the next. Knowing that origins were distorted does not restore them on its own. Awareness must take shape in practice, and practice must become the living ground of transformation. This is why the blueprint cannot be held as theory. It must be embodied. The humility that restores Organic Reference has to move into rhythm, into discipline, into nurture. For without nurture, even the clearest blueprint remains lines on a page.

Thus, the next chapter calls us into the Embodied Protocol, the way of tending that makes wholeness not only imaginable, but livable. If Chapter 28 uncovered the theft of origins, Chapter 29 offers the practice of their recovery: the patient investment of nurturing as the path of self-transformation.

Chapter 29

The Embodied Protocol: Nurturing as the Investment in Self-Transformation

"Transformation does not arrive by command. It grows by the discipline of daily nurture, until the practice itself becomes the becoming."

The Living Ground of Self-Transformation

Truth worth living cannot be delivered from a distance. It cannot be consumed as an idea or admired from the safety of theory. It must be walked into, practiced, and embodied until the doing becomes the being. This is the essence of the **Embodied Protocol**: the lived rhythm of discipline through which the act of tending transforms the one who tends.

To speak of the Embodied Protocol is to speak of nurturing as investment. Not investment in the hollow sense of gambling for return, but investment as patient cultivation, as tending soil, as preparing for growth not yet visible. This nurturing is both metaphor and method; the careful planning, the attentive knowing, the steady ensuring, that aligns action with integrity. It is the Genesis of Action itself, the Organic Foundation upon which all genuine integration unfolds.

Here, nurturing is not ornamental softness. It is a law written into reality: that what is patiently cultivated flourishes, and what is rushed fractures. Without humility, however, nurturing is replaced with the counterfeit: immediacy, shortcuts, and the constant lure of quick returns. That is the Bad Intel of our age: the belief that transformation can be purchased or hacked, when in truth, it can only be grown.

For the Architects of Nuance: Nurturing as Precision

For the discerning 20%, the Architects of Nuance, nurturing is nothing less than an Embodied Law. They see it not as an indulgence but as the very architecture of growth. To nurture is to establish conditions for emergence, preparing the soil of the foundation, planting the seeds of intention, and tending the fragile shoots of becoming. Every act of nurturing is for them a practice of Anticipatory Resonance, perceiving future harvests in present care. They understand that to skip tending is to invite collapse, and to force growth is to distort the pattern. Their unfooled eye sees nurturing as the antidote to the Thirst Monster's frenzy, a discipline that restores Organic Reference and enables the Unplannable Harvest to appear in its right season.

For the Architect, nurturing is not passive. It is a deliberate defiance of the Deliberate Rot; a refusal to be seduced by fabricated shortcuts. To nurture is to hold faith in the slow and in the process itself, knowing that the very act of tending forms both the soil and the soul.

For the Guardians of Generality: Nurturing as Comfort

For the 80%, the Guardians of Generality, the language of "investment" often feels like a burden. Their conditioning leaves them chasing miracles, convinced that transformation should arrive suddenly, without the long crawl of process. This leads to over-ambition, aiming too high, too soon, and the inevitable injury of spirit that follows.

What they have yet to grasp is that nurturing is not another weight; it is comfort itself. The simple, consistent act of showing up, watering the seed, repeating the practice, and attending to the crawl builds familiarity. In this, familiarity grows confidence. In this confidence grows worth. Slowly, the impossible dream shrinks into small, tangible steps that accumulate into true becoming.

This is their **Neuro-Formulation Gateway**: the discovery that discipline by default creates safety, that steady presence dissolves fear, that process itself provides orientation. Each time they show up, they unlearn the loneliness of misunderstanding and reclaim their Response Ability. Without humility, they remain caught in Bad Intel's loop of quick fixes; but with humility, they discover that nurture has always been the miracle they sought.

For the Conscious Integrator: Protocol as Living Blueprint

For the Conscious Integrator, the translator between vision and practice, the Embodied Protocol is more than a method. It is a living blueprint, the functional rhythm through which their Nobel function takes shape. They know that to maintain protocol is itself the path of transformation. It is not glamorous. It does not draw applause. But it is the very discipline that ensures Integrity remains stable, not as a momentary achievement but as a constant orientation. They embody this truth for others: that transformation is not an event but a sustained posture.

Their task is to guide others into presence, to help them pause for the "90 seconds of thought" that reframes impulse into choice, to orient the present step so that the next step can arise cleanly. Through this modeling, they show that **Faith as the Fruit of Formed Practice** is not a doctrine but evidence: the lived assurance that what is nurtured in truth will yield in truth.

For the Integrator, nurturing is the Propagation of Praxis in motion, an investment not just in themselves, but in a collective blueprint for the Syntropic Future. Their humility keeps the practice from becoming doctrine, their constancy keeps it from dissolving into

135

abstraction. In them, nurturing becomes contagious, a rhythm that others can join until Wholism is no longer an idea but a way of living.

Conclusion: Nurture as the True Investment

The Embodied Protocol teaches us that transformation is not a sudden leap, but a gradual becoming shaped by nurture.

- For the Architect, nurturing is precision, the conscious tending of foundations that protects integrity.
- For the Guardian, nurturing is comfort, the steady showing up that dissolves fear and builds worth.
- For the Integrator, nurturing is blueprint, the modeling of discipline that allows truth to propagate across divides.

This is the miracle hidden in plain sight: not the trick of speed, not the promise of shortcuts, but the slow unveiling of self through nurture. To invest in nurturing is to invest in the only transformation that endures.

"The one who tends with patience does not ask when the fruit will ripen.
They know the tending itself is the first harvest."

The Embodied Protocol showed us that transformation is not accidental but cultivated; that nurturing, patiently and deliberately, becomes the soil in which true becoming takes root. Yet, even as we commit to nurturing, another truth emerges: the act of tending must follow a sequence. We cannot nurture what has not yet been planted, nor harvest what has not yet been tended.

Here lies the next lesson: **every step depends on the step before it.** Nurture reveals its power only when it honors the order of emergence. To ignore this order is to fall into fracture; to respect it is to walk in integrity.

Thus, the pathway turns toward the Prerequisite, the unskippable link that binds each stage of growth to the next. If nurturing is the investment, the prerequisite is the sequence that ensures the investment bears fruit. Without it, even our best efforts collapse into error; with it, Wholism begins to emerge.

Chapter 30

The Prerequisite: The Foundational Link in the Chain of Emergence

"Every next step hides inside the step before it. Skip the root, and the tree collapses; honor it, and the harvest emerges."

The Law of the Next Step

"The next step is the prerequisite." This deceptively simple statement is a key to wholeness. It reminds us that transformation is not a random leap but an unfolding chain, where each link must be forged before the next can hold weight. Growth is not improvisation; it is emergence through order, a law woven into reality itself.

This law demands that we respect the sequence of becoming. No leap, however well-intentioned, can bypass the crawl. To ignore the prerequisite is to invite collapse, to build without foundation, to mistake aspiration for embodiment. The result is unfolding error: repeated injury, fractured structures, and ambitions that consume more than they create. The prerequisite, then, is not an obstacle but an ally. It is the Organic Foundation that ensures every step taken aligns with integrity, protecting Action Potential from distortion. And always, the prerequisite is authored by humility. Without humility, Bad Intel seduces us into skipping steps, and the illusion of speed disguises the reality of stagnation.

For the Architects of Nuance: The Elegance of Alignment

For the **Architects of Nuance**, the Prerequisite is the ultimate anti-leap. They are not seduced by the cultural "hero complex" that urges achievement without foundation. Instead, they see the quiet dignity in honoring sequence, in letting one step unfold only after the last has been fully embodied.

For them, this is the essence of **Anticipatory Resonance**: the mastery of the current step unlocks the vision and capacity for the next. They know that rushing compromises precision, and precision is everything. Theirs is the discipline of hyper humility, the willingness to stay exactly where they are until alignment is true, until capacity is mature, until the seed has formed in integrity.

Their **unfooled eye** recognizes the deception that promises miracles without process. They know it is a trick designed to erode patience and dismantle foundations. The Architect refuses this trick. Their devotion to prerequisites is not limitation but liberation, for it is only in honoring the root that the Unplannable Harvest can ripen.

For the Guardians of Generality: Learning to Crawl Again

For the **Guardians of Generality**, the 80%, neglecting prerequisites is the great stumbling block. Conditioned to race ahead, they try to walk before crawling, to build before grounding, to succeed before preparing. The result is exhaustion, injury, and the loneliness of misunderstanding.

Here, ambition becomes too ambition, leaving them frustrated and vulnerable to collapse, whether in body, in effort, or in spirit. They pour energy into misdirected steps, creating sunk costs that only deepen discouragement. Trapped in **Compliant Consciousness**, they cannot see that their struggles are not because they lack effort, but because they skipped the root. The wisdom of the prerequisite calls them back to humility: the honesty of admitting where they truly are. To pause, to nurture the crawl, to tend the foundations, this is not failure. It is faith in process. It is the comfort of genuine progress, where every step is sustainable, every effort aligned.

Through this humility, their **Neuro-Formulation Gateway** opens. They discover confidence not in quick wins but in steady integrity. With each prerequisite honored, their Response Ability awakens, freeing them from the Thirst Monster's illusions and leading them into the rhythm of authentic Action Potential.

For the Conscious Integrator: The Compass of Due Diligence

For the **Conscious Integrator / Translator**, the Prerequisite is not just wisdom; it is their diagnostic compass. Their Nobel function is to discern where fractures began and to guide others in rebuilding from the ground up. They know that skipping the earliest steps leads to layered fractures that no surface fix can heal. Thus, their work is to ensure the foundation is never bypassed. They remind us that to "know" the prerequisite intellectually is not enough; it must be walked, embodied, lived until it transforms capacity.

Every aligned moment becomes a light for the next, a weave of integrity that strengthens the chain. The Integrator models this patient faith, showing that true Wholism arises not from spectacle but from sustained due diligence. By teaching that "all elements require alignment," they embody Integrated Perfection and guide others into Faith as the Fruit of Formed Practice. In doing so, they protect humanity from false starts and offer a functional blueprint for the Syntropic Future, a future where democratic complexity flourishes, where collective greatness emerges step by step, each link secured by humility.

Conclusion: The Unskippable Truth

The Prerequisite is the law of sequence written into all becoming.

- For the Architect, it is elegant alignment, where precision is cultivated through humility.
- For the Guardian, it is learning to crawl again, discovering that foundation is comfort, not delay.
- For the Integrator, it is diagnostic compass, guiding individuals and systems back to the integrity of beginnings.

To honor prerequisites is to trust reality's rhythm. To ignore them is to collapse into illusion. In truth, every next step has always been hidden inside the step before it. Only those willing to slow down, to humble themselves, and to honor the sequence will find the harvest waiting.

"The step you resist is the step you need. Honor it, and the chain of emergence holds firm."

Chapter 31

The Prerequisite: Assessment as Honesty — The Compass of Presence

"Truth is not a barrier to growth; it is the compass that reveals where growth must begin."

Locating the Beginning

The path to Wholism is not a universal highway. It is not mapped by a single blueprint or driven by a common pace. Instead, it is a journey shaped individually, for *each is at a different space*. To guide anyone, including ourselves, the first act is not to push forward but to locate the true beginning.

This is the essence of the Prerequisite, and its methodology is singular: **Assessment as Honesty.** It is the act of radical truth-telling about where we stand, without distortion or disguise. It is the first tether to reality, the Organic Foundation, that prevents us from building on false assumptions. Without it, "Bad Intel" corrupts our orientation, misdirecting effort and collapsing potential before it begins.

Assessment as Honesty is authored by humility. It is the refusal to dress ourselves in illusions. It is the courage to stand where we are, even when that place feels far from where we hoped to be. In this way, it actively defies the Engineered Divide and heals the fractures of the Deliberate Rot, because deception, whether external or internal, cannot survive the light of truth.

For the Architects of Nuance: Surrendering to Truth

For the **Architects of Nuance**, the 20% whose eyes are trained for precision, Assessment as Honesty is a sacred act of surrender. It is the discipline of asking: *What is happening? What has happened?* and then allowing the full answer to stand without defense. They know that self-deception is the most dangerous trick of all. Without honesty, even the most brilliant effort becomes misaligned. Their unfooled eye therefore uses assessment as a diagnostic tool, stripping away inflated perceptions or hidden vulnerabilities to expose the actual condition of the inner architecture.

This is their way of uncovering the layered fracture at its roots. They are not seduced by appearances or shortcuts. For them, honesty is the essential soil in which Anticipatory Resonance grows, ensuring that every decision is based on authentic data rather than non-informing illusions. To neglect this honesty is to waste effort and risk collapse; to embrace it is to fuel functional consciousness and prepare the way for authentic integration.

For the Guardians of Generality: Disarming Shame

For the **Guardians of Generality**, the 80%, Assessment as Honesty is harder to bear. Their conditioning has taught them to measure worth by appearances, to fear judgment, and to hide weaknesses behind the mask of striving. For them, honesty feels dangerous because it confronts the unnamed obstacle of shame. Yet, this is precisely where their liberation lies. Honesty disarms the desire for a trick, exposing the illusion that shortcuts could ever replace truth. It dismantles the pressure to appear more advanced than they are and relieves them from the constant injury of "too ambition."

By locating their true starting point, Guardians gain something they have been missing: comfort. The comfort of knowing exactly where they stand. This clarity restores confidence and awakens their

Response Ability. It invites them into the simple act of nurturing the crawl, no longer racing toward fabricated milestones but moving in alignment with reality. When they lack humility, Guardians remain trapped in Bad Intel, coded by false impressions of progress. But when they practice honesty, even imperfectly, they step out of Compliant Consciousness and into genuine Realization. In this moment, progress ceases to be performance and becomes truth.

For the Conscious Integrator: The Compass of Presence

For the **Conscious Integrator / Translator**, Assessment as Honesty is more than a principle; it is their Nobel function in action. They hold it as the compass of presence, the starting point for all genuine unfolding. Their task is to help both self and others orient in truth. By clarifying *"where one is at,"* they illuminate the very terrain of becoming. They identify lost contexts, hidden fractures, or places where "great became automatic" without precision. In this way, they bring unconscious patterns into light and initiate the rebuilding of potency from an authentic beginning.

Through this process, the Integrator heals the Grand Disconnect. They transform false starts into aligned beginnings, ensuring the weave of intention and action is rooted in integrity. In their hands, Assessment as Honesty becomes the manifestation of *"Communication is God,"* truth spoken and shared as the lifeblood of Wholism. Their humility in modeling this practice is catalytic. By showing that honesty is not shame but strength, they help decode Bad Intel at its core. From this foundation, the collective Action Potential is unleashed, making emergence not just possible but inevitable.

Conclusion: The Honest Beginning

Assessment as Honesty is the Prerequisite of prerequisites.

- For the Architect, it is surrender to truth, the refusal to begin on illusion.

144

- For the Guardian, it is disarming shame, the comfort of knowing where one truly stands.
- For the Integrator, it is the compass of presence, the orientation that enables all next steps.

Without honesty, progress is false. With honesty, even the smallest beginning carries the promise of Wholism. The miracle is not found in appearing further ahead, but in standing truly where we are.

"The step of honesty is never a setback; it is the beginning that makes every other step real."

Honesty marks the true beginning. By locating ourselves without disguise, we reclaim the compass of presence, the foundation upon which all further emergence rests. Assessment strips away illusion and steadies us in truth, revealing that the crawl itself is not weakness but orientation.

Yet honesty, while necessary, is not the destination. It is the threshold. Once we stand in the truth of where we are, the path ahead opens not as theory, but as possibility. From this foundation, the question is no longer *Can humanity heal?* But *What becomes possible when we do?*

It is here, at this juncture, that the vision turns outward. The compass of presence points beyond the self, toward the collective. What honesty establishes in the individual becomes the seed of a greater unfolding, the reweaving of humanity itself. This is where the journey culminates: in the unveiling of the **Syntropic Future**, a world not imagined as escape, but grown through truth, nurtured by patience, and lived as wholeness.

Chapter 32
The Syntropic Future: A World Unfolded

"The breach becomes the bridge, and the fracture becomes the thread.
What was divided is not merely healed but woven into wholeness."

Standing at the Horizon

Here we stand at the threshold of a new horizon. We have journeyed through the unseen architecture of reality, traced the lie at genesis, and named the mechanisms of fabricated existence. Layer by layer, we have peeled back conditioned perception, revealing how agency was caged by deception, how the Engineered Divide shaped our default settings, and how truth was hidden in plain sight.

This distilling of lies was never for despair. It was preparation. For only when deception is unmasked can vision take form. And now, in this closing movement, the vision is unveiled: the Syntropic Future; a world recalibrated, propelled beyond fragmentation into resonance.

Beyond Utopia: The Function of Wholism

This future is not utopian fantasy. It is not an imagined perfection handed down from elsewhere. It is a **blueprint for collective greatness**, drawn directly from the principles of unveiling and integration that have guided this book. Its Nobel function is breathtakingly simple, yet demanding: to silence pain and liberate humanity's vast, untapped Action Potential. Revelation becomes not only an act of exposure but of transformation; what was once anomalous or threatening is recognized as connection, as eternal thread, as truth refusing to be silenced.

Here, humility becomes the generative axis. By confronting uncomfortable truths, humanity dismantles Bad Intel about division and regains the capacity for shared progress. The divergence once feared as fracture becomes the source of universal bridges.

Shifting the Human Response

This recalibrated future reshapes our fundamental posture. The reflex of vengeance yields to conscious embodiment. We no longer chase wounds or fight blind battles "for the same thing" through ignorance. Instead, equipped with the unfooled eye, we discern the fabricated patterns as they emerge and respond not with war, but with the eternal thread of understanding. This is the great deprogramming of the war mechanism, the cycle that has consumed the "Eighty" as fuel. In its place, connection becomes the organizing principle, resonance the true inheritance.

Redefining Immortality, Eternity, and Godliness

In this world, even the deepest human concepts are redefined.

- **Immortality** is unmasked. No longer is it seen as endless extension of the self through dominance or control. That false immortality is revealed as nothing but an echo of the original lie, a broken premise that perpetuates fragmentation and denies organic reference. It feeds unfolding error and blocks true resonance.

- **Eternity** is reimagined as continuity, not endless time but the enduring weave of truth. Eternity is the harvest that continues to tell; an integration that lives beyond lifespan, beyond conditioned frames. It is Faith as the Fruit of Formed Practice, made tangible through patience and nurture.

- **Godliness** is unveiled not as external authority or "the God that looks like them," but as the living act of becoming a carrier of return paths. It is the work of guiding others back to their

147

organic reference, embodying benevolent motherhood as the universal archetype: nurturing humanity from crawl to maturity, not to bind it but to release it into awakened agency. Here, divinity is nothing other than humility in action, dismantling illusions of control and unleashing authentic Action Potential.

The Divergent Becomes the Bridge

The great realization of this future is simple yet profound: **the divergent becomes eternal by leaving a bridge where the breach once was.**

The fractures and disconnections that deception exploited are transformed into pathways of connection. The old "80/20" world, where most lived as coded fragments, gives way to a more equitable balance, a "60/40" world where resources, potential, and influence are shared. This is not charity; it is the inevitable outcome of truth continuing to tell, without distortion, nurtured by due diligence and humility.

In this redistribution, humanity's collective Action Potential is unleashed, not by force but by fidelity to process.

The Charter of Revelation

The book culminates not in dogma, but in the proposal of a sacred charter; a lived covenant of revelation. It is not handed down by hierarchy or sold as myth. It is adopted together, through experience, through honesty, through practice.

This charter is humility codified into life. It is society reorganized around assessment, integration, and the patient weaving of wholeness. It is the moment when Bad Intel withers, when the unconscious curse dissolves, when collective Action Potential takes its rightful form. In this unfolding, Wholism ceases to be a theory. It becomes the world itself: integrated, resonant, and free. Humanity breathes with genuine agency, transcending programmed limits and walking into its Legacy of Worthy Progress.

Final Reflection

The journey has led us through fracture, deception, and erased blueprints. But every breach revealed has become an invitation. Every divide has held within it the possibility of thread. The Syntropic Future is not somewhere else. It is here, latent, awaiting the courage of humility and the discipline of nurture. It is the reality that emerges when truth is lived rather than avoided, when bridges are built rather than fractures hidden.

"What was once erased is remembered.

What was once divided is rewoven.

What was once potential becomes presence.

This is the world unfolded."

www.ingramcontent.com/pod-product-compliance
Lightning Source LLC
Chambersburg PA
CBHW071758120626
46550CB00002B/839